QUESTIONS ON EVERYDAY CHEMISTRY

Peter Borrows

Blackie

ISBN 0-216-92395-6

First published 1988
© Peter Borrows 1988

Illustrated by Mark Bennett

Published by Blackie and Son Ltd
Bishopbriggs, Glasgow G64 2NZ
7 Leicester Place, London WC2H 7BP

British Library Cataloguing in Publication Data

Borrows, Peter
  GCSE questions on everyday Chemistry
  1. Chemistry—Examinations, questions, etc.
  I. Title
  540'76   QD42
  ISBN   0-216-92395-6
                                        Dec 1987

Filmset by Advanced Filmsetters (Glasgow) Ltd.
Printed in Great Britain by Thomson Litho Ltd., East Kilbride, Scotland

► TO THE TEACHER

The GCSE National Criteria for Chemistry place a heavy emphasis on the everyday applications and uses of chemistry, and its social, economic, environmental and technological implications. That is the starting point for each of the questions in this book. Following an initial piece of 'stimulus' material, some questions expect students to be able to recall knowledge, but most demand higher skills of understanding, evaluation and application. Students may be asked to devise practical investigations, or to show their skills at data analysis and communication in a variety of ways, including writing to the press. In some respects, the book complements the 'Science and Technology in Society' materials produced by the Association for Science Education, and it could be used to consolidate ideas met through the use of such materials.

The book will be useful for all GCSE chemistry syllabuses (since all syllabuses must comply with the National Criteria), although it should be especially relevant for those which have emphasized these approaches as a part of their philosophy, e.g. Salter's Chemistry, and the various Nuffield syllabuses. It will also be useful for those teaching the chemistry component of balanced double certificate science syllabuses, such as Nuffield Coordinated Science.

Students may need reassurance when tackling questions that do not depend on recall or routine application. 'I haven't been taught that!' is a common complaint. Some teachers encourage students to respond by giving a mark for an answer—*any* answer—and then adding on further marks for its correctness. Indeed, for some items there is no single correct answer, and this should be made clear to students. Be prepared to give marks for any plausible answer, and to discuss with the class the range of responses produced to the more open-ended questions.

The questions are arranged so that harder ones are towards the end of the book, and to some extent, those on related topics are grouped together, although this has not always been possible. In order to help teachers locate items on particular topics, a cross-referenced index to the National Criteria Core Content has been included.

▶ HINTS FOR THE STUDENT

The advice that follows will help you to answer the questions in this book, and it should also give you some useful tips for answering similar questions in GCSE science exams.

1 The number of marks given for each part of a question indicates how detailed an answer is expected. To gain 3 marks, an answer should normally contain 3 or 4 marking points, or pieces of information. Questions which begin 'What...' or 'Which...' can often be answered in a single sentence, but those which start 'Explain...' need more detail.

2 Many of the questions will relate to experiments you have not done, or chemistry you have not met in the laboratory. You are not expected to have come across these things before—so don't blame your teacher! However, from what you have done, you should be able to apply your knowledge and make a good guess. Don't leave questions blank—that *must* score zero. An answer—any answer—might just be right, even if you're not sure (or even if you think it's wrong).

3 Some questions ask you to devise or describe a possible investigation or experiment. In many cases, this will mean that you should:
- say what equipment you would use (a good diagram saves a lot of writing);
- say what you would do with the equipment, and how you would go about doing it;
- mention any special precautions (e.g. for safety, or to improve accuracy);
- state what you would expect to happen;
- make it clear how you would make any test fair, by controlling variables;
- explain how you would interpret the expected results.

4 If asked why an experiment did not work as expected, *never* say: 'Because of dirty apparatus' or simply: 'Experimental error'. Always assume clean, leak-free equipment, and aim to identify the *causes* of the experimental errors.

5 When drawing diagrams, always use a pencil, and label the parts of the diagram clearly. Normally, you should mention only the apparatus likely to be found in a school laboratory. A stencil is a useful way of quickly producing neat diagrams of about the right size. Stencils are perfectly acceptable to examiners. Avoid using correction fluids.

6 When drawing graphs, always use a pencil. Draw the axes with a ruler, and make sure they are labelled (including units). Similarly, make a neat job of drawing any tables: use a ruler to get straight lines. Remember to head columns with the appropriate title and units.

7 You can use a calculator for any question in this book, but remember to show all steps in your working. You can often get part marks (or even full marks) for a wrong answer, provided your reasoning is clear and along the right lines. Do not give an answer to eight decimal places just because your calculator can. Your answer will be no more accurate than the least accurate part of the data you used to work it out: this will usually be to three figures only.

8 On the whole, examiners are not greatly concerned about how neat your writing is—but they must be able to read it! If reading it takes some time, then they may not bother to read it very carefully. Similarly, there is no need to worry about a few spelling mistakes, as long as your meaning is clear. But, for example, confusing sulph*ate* and sulph*ite*—whether through poor writing or bad spelling—is a major chemical error, and clearly wrong.

9 Always make sure you use all the data available to you. Exam. questions often have lists of data at the start of a question, or on the front cover of the exam. paper. In this book, relative atomic masses and atomic numbers are given on the periodic table at the back of the book. There is also a list of E-numbers for food additives. Use this information whenever it would be helpful to you.

▶ CONTENTS

► ACKNOWLEDGEMENTS

The author and publishers wish to thank the following for their assistance.

Perrier (UK) Limited
Tate and Lyle Sugars
The Walter Kidde Company Limited
H J Heinz Company Limited
Tesco
Silver Spring Mineral Water Company Limited
Volkswagen Audi UK Limited
Extel Financial Limited
Chemical Industries Association Limited
ASL Lane Limited
DDD Limited
Inner London Education Authority
British Gas
Lyons Maid Limited
Birds Eye Wall's Limited
The Solid Fuel Advisory Service
Ethanol Company Limited (Malawi)
Esso
Borough of High Peak
Thermos Limited
Richardson-Vicks Limited
Alphabet Design Partnership
Beecham Toiletries
Melitta Limited
Reckitt and Colman
Harvey Softeners Limited
Premier Brands UK Limited
Corporation of London
BP Oil Limited
ICI Fertilizers
Lawes Fertilizers
Britvic Corona Limited

The Guardian
The Observer
The Daily Telegraph
Times Newspapers Limited
Daily Mirror
Harlow and Epping Star
Chemistry in Britain

▶ 1 VOLVIC WATER

Volvic is a natural mineral water, collected from a spring in the Auvergne region of France.

1   Draw a labelled diagram to show the normal water cycle. Which parts of the normal water cycle can you identify on the labels from this bottle of Volvic water?   *(3 marks)*

Deep under the harsh, deserted volcanic landscape of the Auvergne, in Central France, lies this region's precious natural resource – natural Volvic mineral water.

2   What is meant by a 'porous rock'?   *(1 mark)*

3   What would be the effect of rain water passing through 'fine porous rocks'?   *(1 mark)*

4   Granite is *not* a porous rock. Look at the diagram of the Volvic spring, and explain what will happen to the rain water as it soaks into the ground.   *(2 marks)*

5   The Volvic analysis shows that various different substances are present. Where do these come from?   *(1 mark)*

6   Which metal is most abundant in Volvic water?   *(1 mark)*

7   If you drank a litre of Volvic water, what mass of metals would you consume?   *(1 mark)*

The special geological conditions, created thousands of years ago in the Auvergne, formed a pattern of alternating strata of fine porous rocks and the hardest volcanic stone, through which the mountain springs have created their own natural channels, purifying the water naturally and imparting a unique delicate mineralisation.

Volvic Spring

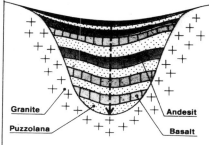

Aqualac (Spring Waters) Ltd.
Part of the PERRIER Group
6 Lygon Place
LONDON SW1W OJR

The water your body needs

We consume up to 220 gallons of water every year. Such is the importance of the water we choose for our family's refreshment. Volvic is authorised and officially recognised as a "Natural Mineral Water." Not all water reaches this standard.

Volvic Analysis

Milligrammes per litre · **Milliequivalents per litre.**

Calcium	10.4	**0.52**	Chlorides	7.5	**0.21**
Magnesium	6	**0.50**	Nitrates	4	**0.06**
Sodium	8	**0.35**	Sulfates	6.7	**0.14**
Potassium	5.4	**0.13**	Bicarbo.	64	**1.04**

Silica 30 mg/l · Total dry extract (mineral content) at 180 °C 110 mg/l · Total hydrotimetric titer 5.2 (French) English H.d. 3.7.

Volvic is suitable for a low sodium diet.

3 057640 100178

▶ **2   WINE BOMB**

Home brewing has become very popular in recent years, but it is not without its dangers, as the story from the *Guardian* newspaper shows.

Wine goes like a bomb

Amateur wine-treaders in Liverpool were warned yesterday that their souvenir bottles of Chateau de Mersey wine might prove rather more memorable than expected.

Last Sunday a chain of Liverpool off-licences organized a treading at the city's international garden festival.

Some 350 visitors leaped about in vats at the vineyard and were then presented with corked and capped bottles of the resulting purplish 'wine'.

The jokey Chateau de Mersey label carried the warnings: 'Produced solely for fun; not to be consumed until the year 3000' but the Cellar 5 company had forgotten the power of fermenting grape.

At breakfast-time yesterday, the first bottle exploded in Skelmersdale. Shortly afterwards a second one went up in Manchester.

Mrs Sheila Bowker, buyer for Cellar 5, said: 'We had no idea that anything like this would happen. We watered the grape juice down after the treading and it was properly corked on a sort of miniature assembly line.

'Anyone who did any treading was given a free bottle. We had a fountain as well, and towels, so that they could wash their feet.'

The two reported explosions involved bottles which had been taken into warm kitchens, accelerating the fermentation of fragments of grape.

Exceptional pressure built up because as well as being corked, the bottles were sealed with plastic caps.

The grapes used were mature purple bunches brought in from outside, as those in the festival vineyard were too few for 350 pairs of feet.

No one was injured by either blast but the circumstances at Skelmersdale were dramatic, according to Mrs Bowker.

'The man involved was having breakfast in the kitchen at the time. He heard this strange noise from the bottle and luckily ducked. Immediately afterwards, the bottle went up.'

Guardian, 20 September 1984
(by Martin Wainright)

1   **(a)** Which chemical, present in grape juice, would actually ferment? *(1 mark)*
    (b) What else, apart from this chemical, is needed for fermentation to take place? *(1 mark)*

2   Two products form when fermentation takes place.
    (a) One of these is a gas: what is its name? *(1 mark)*
    (b) What is the name of the other product? *(1 mark)*

3   **(a)** Explain carefully why the bottles exploded. *(2 marks)*
    (b) Why was there a particular problem with bottles that were kept in a warm kitchen? *(2 marks)*

4   Suppose you wanted to measure the volume of gas produced during the fermentation of one bottle of this 'wine'. Draw a labelled diagram of the apparatus you would use. Explain how you would use the apparatus safely. *(3 marks)*

▶ 3 BROWN SUGAR

Many people like Demerara sugar (often called brown sugar) with their coffee.

1   Demerara sugar is partly-purified cane sugar. In addition to sugar itself, it contains molasses, which is brown in colour. Given this packet of sugar, how would you attempt to find out if the brown pigment is soluble in water or not? Describe carefully what you would do, what you would look for, and how you would explain your observations.   *(3 marks)*

2   If you wash up some coffee cups, you often find sugar left on the bottom. This might be because:
   (i) the person put in too much sugar;
   (ii) the person did not stir it enough.
   (a) Why might sugar be left in the bottom if it was not well stirred?   *(1 mark)*
   (b) Why might sugar be left in the bottom if 'too much' was used?   *(1 mark)*
   (c) How would you try to find out which of the reasons, (i) or (ii), is the correct one? Say what you would do, what you would look for, and how you would interpret your results.   *(3 marks)*

▶ 4 ROSE PETALS

The picture shows a rose.

1   If this was a red rose, how would you attempt to make a concentrated solution of the red pigment in its petals? Describe what you would do, what equipment you would need, and how you would find the best solvent to use.   *(4 marks)*

2   Once you had obtained a suitable solution, how would you test it in order to see if it functioned as an indicator?   *(3 marks)*

▶ 5 DEATH IN A SILO

Compare these two accounts of the same accident, published in two different newspapers. You need to read both in order to get a good picture of what happened.

Farmer and son die in silo

FARMER Crawford Perkins died trying to rescue his son, who fell into a grain silo.

Both were gassed by fumes given off by tons of fermenting barley.

David Perkins, 31, climbed into the 20 ft container to clear a blockage but was overcome by the fumes and toppled from his ladder. His 63-year-old father then climbed in to save him.

Firemen found them lying side by side on top of the grain at Church House Farm, near Hereford.

Daily Mirror, 31 December 1986

Farmers killed in silo

Farmworkers are being urged to stay out of moist grain storage towers following the deaths of a father and son overcome by a build-up of carbon dioxide in a 20-feet high silo.

Mr Crawford Perkins, 63, and his son Crawford David Perkins, 31, were found amid tons of grain. Mr Perkins senior, went into the half-full silo to rescue his son who had climbed inside to examine a fault at Church House Farm, Morton on Lugg, near Hereford, on Monday.

Daily Telegraph, 31 December 1986

1   What gas killed the two men? *(1 mark)*

2   How would you carry out a simple test to see if there was any of this gas in a silo? *(1 mark)*

3   Is this a poisonous gas? How did it kill the men? *(2 marks)*

4   How did this gas get into the silo? *(1 mark)*

5   One report suggests that the barley was fermenting. What chemical change takes place during fermentation? *(2 marks)*

6   Neither newspaper report gives a full scientific explanation of what happened. Re-write the story, explaining the chemistry in a way which a newspaper reader could understand. *(3 marks)*

▶ 6 TEA BAG

The photograph shows a British Rail tea bag.

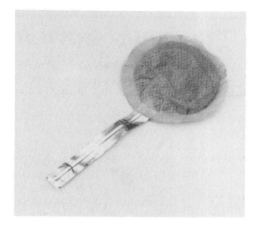

1　The tea leaves are inside the bag, which is made of paper. How does the tea get outside? *(1 mark)*

2　This tea bag has a strip of metal to act as a handle, so that the bag can be moved around in the hot water. Why is it an advantage to be able to move the bag around? *(1 mark)*

3　You might think it is *not* a very good idea to have a strip of metal as the handle for a tea bag which is to be put into hot water. What disadvantage does metal have? *(1 mark)*

4　Suppose you were choosing a suitable metal to make the handle for this tea bag.

  (a) Make a list of the desirable properties that the chosen metal should have (for example, it must not melt in hot water). *(4 marks)*

  (b) Put a tick against those metal properties that you would expect to be able to find in a reference book, and a cross against those for which you would have to carry out a practical investigation. Put a question mark if you are not sure. (For example, you could find the melting point of a metal in a book, so 'melting point' would be a tick). *(2 marks)*

  (c) Choose one of the properties you have marked with a cross. Describe what experiments you would carry out to see if aluminium performed satisfactorily. Give details of what you would do, how you would do it, and what you would look for. *(3 marks)*

► 7 A LIFE-SAVING GAS

This story appeared in *The Times* newspaper.

Soft drink gas could save lives

A gas cylinder normally used to put the fizz into soft drinks could save the lives of miners, industrial workers and lone yachtsmen.

A cylinder of oxygen fitted to a new lightweight breathing bag could provide a 30-minute supply of air to victims of smoke, fumes or poisonous gas. That could just be enough to get them to fresh air and safety.

In the case of mining and industrial accidents, which often involve air poisoning, the best precaution is to provide every man with his own breathing apparatus. Conventional equipment, however, resembles that used by skin divers. It is too heavy, cumbersome and expensive.

Soft drinks cylinders, however, weigh barely a pound as they are stamped out of a single thin disc of metal. They are extremely strong, safe and leak proof—ideal portable breathing apparatus down mines.

In an emergency, a miner pulls a mouthpiece from a safety box at his side and that activates the oxygen bottle and inflates a plastic bag. As he breathes, poisonous carbon dioxide is extracted to keep the air sweet in the bag until the oxygen cylinder gives out.

Another fresh application for the cylinder is in a compact, self-inflating liferaft, now in production by Sea Sure Safety and Survival, of Aldershot. Self-inflating rafts are usually large, heavy and expensive.

The Jon Buoy, however, is so compact and lightweight that it can be carried by the smallest yacht and it not only provides support for the victim, it also insulates him against the cold. The victim can even be winched up by a special lifting ring if he is too weak to move when rescued.

The Times, 29 September 1986

---

1 **(a)** The gas normally found in soft, fizzy drinks is not oxygen: what is it? *(1 mark)*

(b) What would be the effect on somebody if they breathed normal 'fizz-gas' for 30 minutes? Explain your answer carefully. *(2 marks)*

2 Why do victims of smoke, etc., need a supply of oxygen? *(1 mark)*

3 Write a letter to *The Times*, explaining why you don't think very much of their headline. *(3 marks)*

4 Suppose you were given a cylinder of 'life-saving gas'. How would you test to see if it was, in fact, oxygen or normal 'fizz-gas'? Describe what you would do, how you would do it and how you would interpret the results. *(3 marks)*

▶ 8 CONKERS

This letter appeared in *Chemistry in Britain*, the journal of the Royal Society of Chemistry.

1   What are the main chemicals present in vinegar?
(2 marks)

2   How would you investigate whether soaking in vinegar and baking does improve the toughness of conkers? Describe carefully what you would do, and how you would interpret the results. Be sure to indicate how you would make your investigation fair. *(4 marks)*

3   How would you extend your investigation to see whether other processes might be even better? What possibilities would you consider? *(4 marks)*

▶ 9   SALT FOR THE ROADS

The photograph shows a common roadside object.

1   What is the purpose of having salt available at the roadside? *(1 mark)*

2   The salt bins contain crushed rock salt, which contains earthy impurities.

   (a) How is rock salt obtained? *(1 mark)*

   (b) How would you obtain pure salt crystals from a handful of rock salt from this bin? Say what you would do, how you would do it, and what equipment you would use. *(3 marks)*

   (c) At what stage during the process you have just described do the earthy impurities become separated from the salt? *(1 mark)*

3   One reason for putting salt on to the roads might be that it makes ice melt. How would you investigate whether this is correct? If it is correct, how would you then find out the best amount of salt to use to remove ice? *(4 marks)*

Conker query

From Dr Colin McNae

My son is currently soaking horse chestnuts in vinegar, and will shortly bake them, all this to improve their toughness for the game of conkers.

Does any reader know if this time-honoured process achieves its object? In the light of modern chemical knowledge, are there other processes which might improve the toughness of conkers?

From *Chemistry in Britain*

► 10 RECYCLING GLASS

Many towns now have 'bottle banks' where old glass bottles can be collected for recycling.

1   **(a)** What is meant by recycling?   *(1 mark)*
       (b) Why is recycling considered a good idea?   *(2 marks)*

2   **(a)** Why do you think that bottle tops and other pieces of metal should *not* be thrown into the skips?   *(1 mark)*
       (b) Why do you think it necessary to collect the clear and coloured glass bottles separately?   *(1 mark)*

3   Clear glass is made by heating silicon dioxide with sodium and calcium carbonates.
       (a) If coloured glass is required, then small amounts of certain metal oxides are added. From your knowledge of the periodic table, which metal oxides are likely to be suitable?   *(1 mark)*
       (b) How would you investigate the best proportions in which to mix silicon dioxide and sodium and calcium carbonates, in order to produce a glass capable of resisting attack by acids and alkalis? Describe what you would do, how you would do it, what you would look for, and how you would interpret your results.
                                   (4 marks)

▶ 11 ACID SPILL

Road accidents involving chemicals happen from time to time, and the emergency services always have plans ready to deal with them. Read the report of an accident involving hydrochloric acid.

1 You have probably used hydrochloric acid in your school laboratory without wearing breathing apparatus. Why do you think the fire-fighters needed to wear breathing apparatus?
(1 mark)

2 What type of chemical must soda ash be, if it was used to neutralize the acid? *(1 mark)*

3 How could you know when enough soda ash had been added? *(1 mark)*

4 Soda ash is impure sodium carbonate.
  (a) From what raw materials would you expect soda ash to be made? *(1 mark)*
  (b) Why do you think soda ash was chosen, rather than other possible chemicals which could neutralize the acid? *(1 mark)*

5 Why do you think it was necessary to neutralize the acid? Why not just wash it away with water? *(1 mark)*

6 Suppose you were the journalist who wrote this story, and you decided to write a few more sentences to explain to the general reader why the acid was neutralized, and how neutralization worked. What would you write? *(4 marks)*

▶ 12 FIRE EXTINGUISHER

Look at the photograph of a common type of fire extinguisher.

1 How does this type of extinguisher put out a fire? *(1 mark)*

2 What forces the water out of the extinguisher? *(1 mark)*

3 **(a)** Why do the instructions say that this extinguisher is not for use on electrical fires? *(2 marks)*
  (b) Why do the instructions say that it is not for use on burning liquids? *(2 marks)*
  (c) Suppose a chip pan caught fire at home. How would you deal with it? Explain your reasons. *(2 marks)*

FIREMEN TACKLE ACID SPILL

FIREMEN wearing breathing apparatus tackled a spillage of hydrochloric acid at STC in West Road on Thursday.

The acid had leaked from a drum on the back of a lorry but no one was hurt. Firemen used soda ash to neutralize the small spillage and washed down the surrounding area. Three appliances attended the incident.

Harlow and Epping Star,
13 February 1986

19

▶ 13 SALT IN CHESHIRE

Read the extract from an article on the history of salt.

Salt of the earth

Cheshire is renowned for cheese and a grinning cat. Its salt deposits are less trumpeted. Salt, so crucial an element of life, has long and widely been used as a means of taxation. The story of salt in that part of Cheshire bounded by towns ending in 'wich' makes a fascinating and pleasurable study. The trail links are through soft countryside and rich farming land past picturesque black and white buildings. Start at Nantwich or from Sandbach's stone crosses in the cobbled square.

I like Nantwich exceedingly from the Elizabethan Churche's Mansion, now an excellent restaurant, to the grand church with a choir rich in misericords to finger and decipher. This was the first town in Cheshire to develop salt.

The Romans exploited the stuff and Domesday mentions 'salt-houses'. When the salt works closed in 1882, Snow Hill opened as a brine bath centre offering cures for gout, rheumatism, even insomnia. Nantwich Museum produces a neat summary of events sold with a sachet of salt to prove it.

In this region flashes or lakes, now used for sailing and caused by subsidence from brine pumping, abound. 'Beware Flooding' signs are common on country lanes, but in urban terms it meant cruel devastation of homes and saga-long struggles for compensation. It makes a good geographical and social study.

Rock salt was discovered around Northwich, Cheshire's salt capital, in 1670. Eight mines worked last century. Today only one remains effective, the ICI-owned Meadowbank at Winsford. From here salt was exported as cattle lick. Current production, two and a quarter million tons, goes onto our icy roads.

Times Educational Supplement,
24 February 1984

1 What, from a chemist's point of view, is wrong with the statement, 'Salt, so crucial an element of life...'? *(2 marks)*

2 Why was salt very important in the past? *(1 mark)*

3 '...lakes,...caused by subsidence from pumping brine...'
(a) What is brine? *(1 mark)*
(b) Why was it pumped? *(1 mark)*
(c) Why would this cause subsidence? *(1 mark)*
(d) How would salt be obtained from brine? *(1 mark)*

4 Rock salt is mined today in huge amounts.
(a) Why is salt put on roads? *(1 mark)*
(b) Salt is a very important raw material for manufacturing many other chemicals. List some of the chemicals which are made from salt, indicating why each is important.
(4 marks)

▶ 14 COPPER BEECH LEAVES

The picture shows a leaf from the copper beech tree, which is so called because of the beautiful and unusual copper colour of its leaves.

1   The leaves from most trees are green.
   (a) What is the green pigment called?   *(1 mark)*
   (b) What job does the green pigment do?   *(1 mark)*
   (c) What is the main chemical reaction taking place in green leaves? Say what it is called, and what chemical change takes place.   *(3 marks)*

2   How would you investigate whether copper beech leaves do, in fact, contain a green pigment as well as a red pigment? Say exactly what you would do, what equipment you would use and what you would look for.   *(5 marks)*

▶ 15 LIGHTNING CONDUCTOR

Many tall buildings have lightning conductors like the one shown in this photograph of a church tower.

1   **(a)** Lightning conductors are normally made of copper. Give two reasons why copper is suitable.   *(2 marks)*
   (b) Give three other important uses for copper.   *(3 marks)*

2   Lightning conductors usually appear bright green, due to surface corrosion.
   (a) What evidence is there to suggest that the green stuff is a copper compound?   *(1 mark)*
   (b) How would you use a flame test to confirm that the green stuff does indeed contain copper?   *(2 marks)*
   (c) Some books suggest that the green material is a carbonate. How would you investigate whether this was so?   *(2 marks)*

▶ **16 SPONGE PUDDING**

DIRECTIONS: Place can in a large saucepan containing sufficient boiling water for can to float, at least 2½ pints. Boil gently for 35 minutes. On no account allow to boil dry. Add more water as necessary.

TO OPEN: To prevent spurting, hold cloth over can opener when removing can top marked 'open this end first'. Run a knife around the inside of the can. Turn can over onto a plate, open other end and press out. Made in England. H. J. HEINZ CO. LTD. Hayes, Middx. UB4 8AL.

A can of sponge pudding is a common enough food! It is warmed up before eating by standing the can in a pan of water, and allowing it to boil.

1   At what temperature will the water in the pan boil?
(1 mark)

2   Whilst there is plenty of boiling water in the pan, what will be the temperature of the sponge pudding inside the can?
(1 mark)

3   What would happen to the temperature of the sponge pudding inside the can if the water in the pan boiled dry?
(1 mark)

4   Explain in detail why the label insists that the water in the pan must *not* be allowed to boil dry.   *(2 marks)*

5   Explain why some of the contents might spurt out if the hot can is not opened according to the instructions.   *(1 mark)*

▶ 17 BLEACH

Bleach is perhaps the most dangerous chemical found around the home. Look carefully at the warnings on the bleach bottle label.

IRRITANT

Contains Sodium Hypochlorite.
Contact with acids liberates toxic gas.
Irritating to eyes and skin. Keep out of reach of children. Avoid Contact with eyes.
Keep upright in a cool, safe place.

First Aid: In event of accident, if splashed on skin or eyes, wash thoroughly with water. If inadvertently swallowed, give plenty of milk or water to drink and obtain medical advice. Show this container to the doctor.

DO NOT remove label unless contents are completely used and bottle rinsed out.

DO NOT transfer contents into another bottle.

DO NOT mix with other toilet cleaners, acids or other cleaning products as this could give rise to dangerous fumes (chlorine).

Produced in the UK for Tesco Stores Ltd., Cheshunt, Herts.

INSTRUCTIONS FOR USING CHILD SAFETY CAP
To Open:- 1. Place bottle on a firm flat surface. 2. Press down cap and hold down while screwing anti-clockwise.
To Close:- 1. Place bottle on a firm flat surface. 2. Replace cap and screw on clockwise until tight. 3. Check cap is closed by a reverse turn which should give a click.

DIRECTIONS FOR USE
Toilets: Pour neat around the bowl every night to kill germs and remove stains.
Outside Drains: Pour neat into drains to disinfect and cure all unpleasant smells.
Sinks and Basins: Pour neat down waste pipe. Rinse thoroughly with cold water after 2-3 minutes.
Work Surfaces: Disinfect all surfaces with a solution of Tesco Thick Bleach (½ egg cup p. one gallon of water).
Whites: Mix ¼ egg cup of Bleach per gallon of water, do not put Bleach straight onto fabrics, dilute first. Immerse whites for a short time then rinse thoroughly. If soaking overnight use half strength. (NB. Always consult the garment label before using Bleach on whites). Bleach must not be used for woollens, silks, viscose, modal waffle, seersucker, pique, everglaze, leather, man-made or specially treated materials. Do not use on baths or plated articles. Keep away from carpets and soft furnishings.

5 000119 340948

1 If you were handling sodium hypochlorite solution in your school laboratory, what safety precautions would you expect to adopt? *(1 mark)*

2 Why do you think this bottle has a 'child safety cap'? *(1 mark)*

3 What do you think is the main raw material from which sodium hypochlorite is made? *(1 mark)*

4 'Contact with acids liberates toxic gas.'
   (a) What does 'toxic' mean? *(1 mark)*
   (b) What is this toxic gas? *(1 mark)*

5 'Dangerous fumes' are formed when bleach is mixed with 'other toilet cleaners'. What sort of chemical do you think toilet cleaners might consist of? *(1 mark)*

6 Suppose you wanted to measure the maximum volume of toxic gas you could get by mixing a bottle of bleach with acid. How would you go about it? Draw a labelled diagram of the apparatus you would use. Describe how you would use it, and mention any precautions you would take. *(4 marks)*

Compare the labels from these two fizzy drinks. (Lists of E-numbers are given at the back of this book).

REAL BRITISH COLA DRINK

SILVER SPRING FOLKESTONE ENGLAND

PLEASE UNSCREW GENTLY KEEPING HAND OVER CAP UNTIL PRESSURE IS RELEASED

BOTTLED UNDER AUTHORITY OF ROLA COLA LTD

5 010497 200017

Ingredients: Carbonated Water, Sugar, Caramel, Colouring, Flavourings, Phosphoric Acid, Preservative - Sodium Benzoate, Caffeine, Artificial Sweetener-Saccharin

NO DEPOSIT NO RETURN

2 Litre

TESCO

LOW CALORIE LEMONADE

Sparkling

DIET LEMONADE

e 1½ LITRES

VEET®
END

LESS THAN 1 CALORIE PER LITRE

KEEP COOL
AND OUT OF SUNLIGHT.
PRESSURE CONTAINER,
AVOID DAMAGE TO CAP.

DRINK WITHIN 3 DAYS
OF OPENING.

Can help slimming or weight control only as part of a controlled diet.

Energy value
Per 100 ml (3½ fl. oz)
0.15 kJ (0.03 kcal)
Per 140 ml (¼ pt) serving
0.2 kJ (0.05 kcal)

INGREDIENTS:
WATER, CARBON DIOXIDE, CITRIC ACID, FLAVOURING, ARTIFICIAL SWEETENERS (SACCHARIN, ASPARTAME), PRESERVATIVE (E211)

*Nutrasweet is a trademark of G. D. Searle & Co.

1 Which sweetener is present in both drinks? *(1 mark)*

2 **(a)** Do both drinks contain the same preservative? Give the name(s). *(1 mark)*

(b) Why is a preservative necessary in these drinks?

(1 mark)

3 **(a)** Why do you think the Rola Cola label says, 'Please unscrew gently, keeping hand over cap until pressure is released.'? *(1 mark)*

(b) Diet Lemonade states that it should be kept cool and out of sunlight. Explain what might happen if it was not. *(2 marks)*

4 Approximately what pH would you expect these drinks to have? Why? *(2 marks)*

5 Diet Lemonade stresses that it is a low calorie drink. Explain carefully what the difference is between Diet Lemonade and Rola Cola which makes Diet Lemonade a low calorie drink. *(2 marks)*

6 Some people think that fizzy drinks attack your teeth. How would you investigate whether these two drinks do so, and do so equally? Say what you would do, how you would do it, what you would look for, and how you would interpret your results. *(4 marks)*

▶ 19 FIZZY DRINKS (B)

If you compare the labels of Sparkling Cola Drink and Rola Cola, you will see that they both contain phosphoric acid.

Suppose you were given a solution of an alkali, together with anything else you needed; how would you find which of the two drinks contained the greater amount of phosphoric acid? Say what equipment you would use, how you would carry out your investigation, and how you would interpret your results.

(4 marks)

INGREDIENTS
CARBONATED WATER,
SUGAR,
MALT EXTRACT,
NATURAL FLAVOURINGS,
(INCLUDING EXTRACT
OF COLA NUT),
PHOSPHORIC ACID,
CAFFEINE

ST.CLEMENTS
Sparkling
COLA
DRINK
NO ARTIFICIAL COLOURINGS, SWEETENERS, FLAVOURING, OR PRESERVATIVE

▶ 20 LEMONADE

Carefully study this label from a bottle of lemonade.

NUTRITION		
AVERAGE COMPOSITION	PER 200ml (⅒ Pint) serving	PER 100g (3½ oz)
Energy	176 kJ/42 kcal	88 kJ/21 kcal
Fat	0g	0g
Protein	0g	0g
Carbohydrate	11g	5.5g
Added Sugars	11g	5.5g

INFORMATION

KEEP COOL
AND OUT OF SUNLIGHT.
PRESSURE CONTAINER,
AVOID DAMAGE TO CAP.

**DRINK WITHIN 3 DAYS
OF OPENING.**

INGREDIENTS: CARBONATED WATER, SUGAR, CITRIC ACID, FLAVOURINGS, ACIDITY REGULATOR (SODIUM CITRATE). PRESERVATIVE (E211), ARTIFICIAL SWEETENER (SACCHARIN).

TESCO QUALITY: IF YOU ARE NOT ENTIRELY SATISFIED WITH ANY TESCO PRODUCT PLEASE RETURN IT TO THE STORE WHERE IT WAS PURCHASED, WHERE WE WILL BE PLEASED TO REPLACE IT. OR SEND IT WITH THE PACKAGING TO THE CONSUMER RELATIONS MANAGER AT THE FOLLOWING ADDRESS, STATING WHERE AND WHEN IT WAS PURCHASED. THIS OFFER DOES NOT AFFECT YOUR STATUTORY RIGHTS. PRODUCED IN THE U.K. FOR TESCO STORES LTD., P.O. BOX 18, CHESHUNT, HERTS., EN8 9SL. © TESCO '87.

5 000119 160492

1 Use the lists of E-numbers at the back of this book to find the name of the preservative used in the lemonade. *(1 mark)*

2 **(a)** What does the label mean when it refers to 'carbonated water'? *(1 mark)*

(b) The lemonade is described as 'sparkling'. What gives it the sparkle? *(1 mark)*

(c) Why does the label say that this is a 'pressure container'? *(1 mark)*

(d) The label also says, 'keep cool and out of sunlight'. If the bottle was warmed up, would the dissolved gas inside become more or less soluble? *(1 mark)*

3 Using equipment you would expect to find in a school laboratory, how could you measure the volume of gas which had been dissolved in order to make this 3 litre bottle of lemonade? Draw a labelled diagram of the apparatus you would use, and explain how you would use it. *(3 marks)*

▶ 21 FOOD COLOURS

Compare the labels from the three bottles of food colours.

1   Some children may be affected by tartrazine. Which food colour(s) should they avoid?   *(1 mark)*

2   **(a)** Copy and complete the following equation:

$$\text{solute} + \text{solvent} \longrightarrow \ldots\ldots\ldots$$ *(1 mark)*

   (b) Isopropyl alcohol is used as the solvent in Green Food Colour. What solvent is used in Blue Food Colour?   *(1 mark)*

   (c) Why do you think different solvents are needed for the different food colours?   *(1 mark)*

   (d) What *solute* is used in Yellow Food Colour?   *(1 mark)*

3   Acetic acid is used as a preservative in all these food colours.

   (a) By what name is acetic acid more commonly known?   *(1 mark)*

   (b) Preservatives which are permitted for food use in the EEC must have an E-number. Is acetic acid a permitted preservative? If so, what is its E-number? (See the lists at the end of the book.)   *(1 mark)*

4   How would you show that Blue Food Colour is a mixture of two pigments? Describe what equipment you would use, how you would use it, and what results you would expect.   *(3 marks)*

5   A chromatogram was made using the three food colourings, with the results as shown.

   Which food colour was placed at spot **X**, which at spot **Y**, and which at spot **Z**? Explain how you arrive at your answers.   *(3 marks)*

Chromatogram results:

Food colourings

► 22 RUSTING CARS

Many car makers have attempted to overcome the problems of rust. Read one manufacturer's claims in this advertisement.

Since the invention of the internal combustion engine, rust has been the motor car's No 1 enemy.

And it was a problem Audi was determined to crack with the launch of the new Audi 80.

Over the years, car manufacturers (and Audi in particular) have come up with a number of highly-effective ways of keeping the demon rust at bay.

But rust plays a very long game.

Given time, it seems rust will get its teeth through any painted-on protective layer. Then go on to eat into the metal itself (along with the resale value of your car).

Alone, but for the notable exception of Porsche, Audi invested the money and resources needed to find a radical solution.

As a result, the very sheet metal from which the new Audi 80 is built is first zinc galvanised. To a thickness of 8 microns. And on both sides.

If a stone flies up from the road and hits this car hard enough to chip through the paint, something extraordinary happens.

The zinc 'bleeds' over the bare metal and, in effect, heals the wound.

Of course, as a reader of the motoring press, you'll know there's nothing rusty about the new Audi 80 from any point of view.

Its drag factor of Cd 0.29 is a world best for the class.

And the options list wouldn't disgrace a car twice the price: four-wheel-drive, ABS, fuel injection, leather interior, one-touch electric windows, electric door mirrors and sunroof, air-conditioning.

The new Audi 80 also offers one option not available on any other car in the world.

It's a safety system called Procon-Ten, invented by Audi, and it's designed to help you walk away from the head-on collision none of us likes to think about.

The new Audi 80: it makes other new cars look as if they have quite a few miles on the clock■

1 **(a)** What is the main material from which a car body is made? *(1 mark)*

   (b) Copy the diagram on the left. It represents a section through a car body, showing the layers of materials used in coating it. In place of the letters **A**, **B** and **C** write, in the correct places, the words: *zinc, paint, sheet steel.* *(2 marks)*

2 Why is a coat of paint by itself not sufficient protection from rust? *(1 mark)*

3 Which metal, zinc or steel, would you expect to corrode more rapidly? Why? *(2 marks)*

4 Describe how you would investigate whether the Audi treatment does make cars rust more slowly. Describe what you would do, what equipment you would use, what you would look for, and how you would interpret your results. *(4 marks)*

5 Salt is often put on the roads in winter. Do you think this would affect the speed at which an Audi car rusts? Describe how you would investigate this idea. *(4 marks)*

▶ 23 TIN CAN

This picture shows a 'tin' can that once contained grapefruit.

1 About what pH would you expect the grapefruit juice to be? Why? *(2 marks)*

2 **(a)** Although we often refer to 'tin' cans, they are not, in fact, actually made of tin: there is just a thin coating of tin over another metal. What is this other metal? *(1 mark)*

   (b) What chemical reaction might take place between this other metal and grapefruit juice? *(2 marks)*

   (c) Use your knowledge of the reactivity series to explain how a coating of tin protects the metal. *(2 marks)*

3 You can see the speckled pattern of tin crystals on the inside of the can. How do you think this coating of tin was applied to the other metal? *(1 mark)*

4 If tin is so good, suggest two possible reasons why the entire can is not made out of tin, rather than just using a thin coating. *(2 marks)*

5 It is often suggested that scrap metal, including old tin cans, should be recycled.

   (a) What is meant by recycling? *(1 mark)*

   (b) Why is recycling considered to be a good idea? *(2 marks)*

   (c) Why might it be difficult to recycle the metals in this tin can? *(2 marks)*

There is growing concern about the amount of nitrates found in drinking water. Read the report which appeared in the *Observer*.

BRITAIN TO BE SUED OVER POLLUTED DRINKING WATER

BRITAIN is facing legal action from the Common Market for regularly supplying at least a million people here with polluted drinking water.

Very high levels of the pollution can cause infantile methaemoglobinaemia, or 'blue baby' syndrome. Lower levels are suspected by some scientists of setting off a chain reaction in the body which causes stomach cancer. The European Commission announced last week that it had decided to start formal proceedings, which could lead to the Government being hauled before the European Court.

The Department of the Environment said it had no idea legal proceedings were planned. It will particularly embarrass Environment Ministers, because it is the second case of EEC legal action against them in a few days. Late last week the EEC announced it was beginning legal proceedings over a toxic waste incinerator near Pontypool in South Wales.

The current action arises from levels of nitrates, which come mainly from artificial fertilizer in drinking water.

The EEC's drinking water directive, implemented in 1985, laid down that no drinking water should contain more than 50 mg per litre of nitrate at any time. But large areas of Britain exceed that level. Britain chose to interpret the directive differently, as allowing supplies to exceed that level at times, so long as the *average* pollution over a three-month period stayed beneath it. Even after this manoeuvre—attacked by environmentalists as illegal—it had to admit that 52 water supplies exceed its limits. By its own figures, 921 000 people receive water that averages more than 50 mg a litre over three months.

Most live in Lincolnshire, Cambridgeshire, north Nottinghamshire, north-west Norfolk, Norwich, north Warwickshire, east Worcestershire, and the Lichfield, Leamington Spa, Dudley and Luton areas.

Friends of the Earth calculates that more than five million people receive water that exceeds the true EEC rules, going over the limit at some time. Britain has applied for the 52 supplies to be exempted from the EEC rules—but this is unlikely to be accepted by the Commission. Following at least six complaints from bodies and individuals, it is now starting legal action to force Britain to comply with the directive.

Ironically, the EEC action may strengthen the hand of Mr William Waldegrave, the Government's Green Minister, whose department is the subject of the prosecution. Last year he tried to get the Government to set up special water protection zones, above drinking water sources, where farmers would only be able to use limited amounts of fertilizer, but he was blocked by Mr Michael Jopling, the Agriculture Minister.

Observer, 1 February 1987

1 Give two medical problems which can be caused by too much nitrate in the drinking water. *(2 marks)*

2 What is the maximum amount of nitrate that the EEC considers should be in drinking water? *(1 mark)*

3 The newspaper suggests that Britain manages to get round the EEC regulations. How? *(1 mark)*

4 How does nitrate get into drinking water? *(1 mark)*

5 Why do you think the amount of nitrate in drinking water has increased in recent years? *(1 mark)*

6 Write a letter to the newspaper saying what you think should be done about this problem. Explain carefully any scientific arguments you use. *(4 marks)*

▶ 25 RUSSIAN CHEMISTRY

You probably can't read Russian, but the symbols of chemistry form an international language. This passage comes from a Russian chemistry textbook.

Реакции образования кристаллогидратов, например:

$$CuSO_4 + 5H_2O = CuSO_4 \cdot 5H_2O,$$

являются реакциями экзотермическими. Обратный процесс — обезвоживание кристаллогидратов — требует затраты тепла.
Прочность кристаллогидратов различна. В некоторых случаях они разрушаются уже при комнатной температуре, в других случаях для этого необходимо сильное нагревание.

What do you think this passage is about? Write a few sentences, in such a way that the equation can be sensibly included. *(5 marks)*

▶ 26   THEFT!

This *Guardian* report has a worrying headline.

1   What poison was stolen from the school?   *(1 mark)*

2   Which of the warning symbols below would you expect to find on the bottle of poison?   *(1 mark)*

3   If magnesium really was explosive, which of the warning symbols would you expect to find on its bottle?   *(1 mark)*

4   Write a letter to the newspaper, explaining why you do not think that their knowledge of the chemistry of magnesium is very good.   *(4 marks)*

5   Suppose you discovered that it was somebody in your class who had stolen these chemicals. What would you say to them?   *(3 marks)*

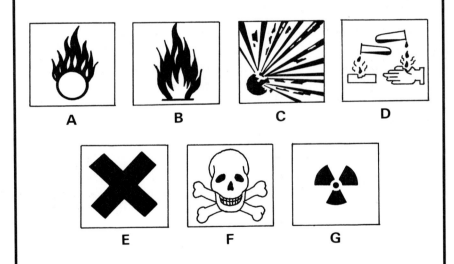

A   B   C   D

E   F   G

▶ 27 FIRE ON DYNAMITE SHIP

In March 1987 a ship loaded with dynamite caught fire and was abandoned by her crew. Read the newspaper report which appeared at the time.

Nitrogen plan to put out fire on freighter

The Danish freighter loaded with dynamite which was abandoned in the Channel seven days ago after a fire, is to be pumped full of nitrogen as soon as the weather improves, coastguards said yesterday.

Salvage men will inject the gas into the hold of the Hornestrand in an attempt to smother whatever fire remains by depriving it of oxygen. But the Dutch salvage tug Typhoon will need calm seas before going alongside the vessel, which has 400 tons of seismic gelatine explosives aboard.

Nitrogen will be pumped into the ship through a pipeline from the Typhoon after men have gone aboard to secure an entry point.

The crew of five, three men and two women, abandoned ship last Tuesday when they noticed smoke and heat rising from fore and aft hold ventilators. The freighter was some 30 miles off the Devon coast at the time, between some of the world's busiest commercial shipping lanes.

British and French naval ships guarded her to keep other vessels away. In the past week, there have been several meetings of salvage and naval experts to decide how best to deal with the emergency.

The Hornestrand, which was bound for West Africa via a number of European ports, was anchored last night off the Cornish coast, where it had been slowly towed by a salvage tug, six miles west of the Eddystone light and nine miles from nearest land.

HMS Achilles and a Dutch tug are keeping other vessels away. It was thought that any fire down below had burnt itself out. But yesterday salvors saw smoke rising again from the freighter, and using infra-red equipment, detected a 'hot spot' in her forward hold.

Commander David Eliot, southwest regional controller of coastguards, said the technical team handling the problem had decided that 'as soon as the weather moderated to calm, it will be necessary to inject a large quantity of nitrogen into the cargo hold to suppress whatever fire is there. At the same time, gas samples of the atmosphere in the hold will be taken for chemical analysis.'

Guardian, 10 March 1987
(by Gareth Parry)

1 **(a)** What three things are necessary for a fire to occur?
(3 marks)

(b) Why would 'depriving the fire of oxygen' put it out?
(1 mark)

2 What is it about nitrogen that made it suitable for fighting this fire?
(2 marks)

3 Give the name of another gas which might have been used in place of nitrogen, and explain why it would have been suitable.
(2 marks)

4 Water is often used to put out fires. Suggest a possible reason why it was not used in this case.
(1 mark)

5 Transporting explosives is obviously rather dangerous.
(a) Which of the signs on page 32 would you expect to find on a container of explosives?
(1 mark)

(b) Why are explosives useful (other than as weapons of war)?
(2 marks)

▶ 28 FIRE EXTINGUISHER DANGER

Read the story of a fire fight that went wrong.

Extinguishers gas 13 in fire

Thirteen people—including five firemen—were poisoned by fumes yesterday when banned fire extinguishers were used to fight a blaze.

The extinguishers gave off invisible phosgene gas—which was used in the First World War.

Three of the sick firemen and four other people were kept in hospital.

The victims began choking and having dizzy spells while the blaze was being put out at the Post Office radio station in Rugby, Warwickshire.

Mr Eric Seager, area engineer at the station—which links countries by radio telephone—said last night: 'A lot of chaps rushed up with extinguishers when the fire broke out.'

'Someone grabbed two or three carbon tetrachloride ones, which mustn't be used on electrical fires. They should have known better.' Station officer Ron Hall, who led the firemen, said: 'The gas choked us although we were wearing breathing apparatus.'

Danger

'It was all right if you kept still, but the moment you moved or got into cold air, you just couldn't breathe.'

The Home Office has warned fire brigades not to use the carbon tetrachloride extinguishers because of the gas danger. They must all be replaced by 1973.

Daily Mirror, 8 December 1971

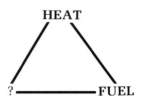

The 'fire triangle'

1   Why would a similar story not appear today?   *(1 mark)*

2   Fire-fighters often talk about the 'fire triangle'.
   (a) Copy this triangle and fill in the gap.   *(1 mark)*
   (b) Use the fire triangle to explain how carbon tetrachloride could put a fire out.   *(2 marks)*

3   Carbon tetrachloride melts at $-23\,°C$ and boils at $77\,°C$.
   (a) What will its physical state be at room temperature?   *(1 mark)*
   (b) Would you expect carbon tetrachloride to be able to conduct electricity? Explain your answer.   *(2 marks)*

4   Carbon tetrachloride, CCl_4, is dangerous on electrical fires because, in contact with hot metal, it may form phosgene, $COCl_2$.
   (a) What else would be needed for phosgene to form?   *(1 mark)*
   (b) What job do you think the hot metal might perform in forming phosgene?   *(2 marks)*

5   Suggest what sort of fire extinguisher might be used safely on an electrical fire, and explain why it is suitable.   *(2 marks)*

▶ 29   METAL PRICES

Prices of metals and other commodities are published every day in the press.

1   Give one important use for each of the *metals* listed.
(4 marks)

2   Silver is listed as 350 p per troy oz. If 1 tonne = 32 000 troy oz, what is the price of silver in £ per tonne?   *(2 marks)*

3   Draw up a table, showing the *cash* price per tonne of the metals (and only the metals). Arrange the metals in order of increasing price.   *(2 marks)*

4   **(a)** One factor which might affect the price of a metal is its scarcity in the Earth's crust. State *three* further factors which could affect the price of a metal.   *(3 marks)*
   (b) This table shows the relative abundance in the Earth's crust of the four metals.

Metal	Abundance
Silver	1
Lead	159
Copper	705
Zinc	1318

Does this support the view that a metal's price might depend upon its abundance in the Earth's crust? Explain your answer.   *(3 marks)*

5   **(a)** Copper is often recycled. What does this mean?
   (2 marks)
   (b) Why is copper recycled? Give at least two reasons.
   (2 marks)

COMMODITIES

Crude oil: Petroleum Argus range for 15 day Brent $ to $.
Copper: Cash £865 per tonne; three months £885 per tonne.
Lead: Cash £310.50 per tonne; three months £302.50 per tonne.
Zinc: Cash £474 per tonne; three months £466 per tonne.
Silver: Cash 350 p per troy oz.; three months 359 p.
Rubber: Spot 61 p per kilo.
Coffee: Mar 1 253 per tonne; May 1 270 per tonne; July 1 290 per tonne; Sept 1 313 per tonne; Nov 1 345 per tonne; Jan 1 375 per tonne.
Cocoa: Mar 1 268 per tonne; May 1 305 per tonne; July 1 334 per tonne; Sept 1 357 per tonne; Dec 1 382 per tonne; Mar 1 406 per tonne.
Cotton: Liverpool prices in US cents per pound. US Memphis $\frac{1}{16}$ inch strict middling, Mar–Apr 63.50; US California $\frac{1}{8}$ inch strict middling, Mar–Apr 77.00; Sudan Baraket 1$\frac{1}{2}$ inch, Mar–Apr No 3b 94.00, Mar–Apr No 5b 87.00, Mar–Apr No 6b 76.50; Mexico 1$\frac{1}{16}$ inch strict middling, Mar–Apr 67.00.

Guardian, 5 March 1987

These are parts of a poster produced by the Chemical Industries Association concerning the transport of chemicals by road. They explain the warning panels which you see on the back and sides of every tanker carrying a hazardous product.

Cracking the Hazchem code

Look at the Hazchem scale (right), together with our real life example for substance 1017-chlorine. In the top panel, we have 2XE. The number tells the fire brigade what to use on a spillage – in this case 2, water fog or spray equipment. X is in the 'contain' half of the table. This material must be prevented, by whatever means possible, from entering drains or watercourses. 'Dilute' means a material can be flushed away, but not this one.

The letter 'X' advises the emergency services to use 'Full', that is full body protective clothing with breathing apparatus. Just 'BA' would mean breathing apparatus with protective gloves. When you see a 'V' next to the letter, it means that a substance can be violently, or even explosively, reactive. 'E' advises the men on the spot to consider evacuation if the accident occurs in a built-up area.

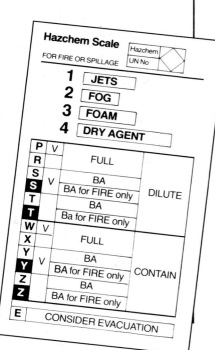

The Black and White marking scheme

For low hazard chemicals which are not covered by regulations, CIA has introduced a voluntary 'black and white marking scheme'. Again this identifies the chemical being carried and gives advice to the emergency services about how to deal with it. It's a scheme which goes beyond the law to give the public extra protection and reassurance.

▶ **30   THE HAZCHEM CODE (A)**

1   (a) On a tanker containing antifreeze, why is there no diamond symbol in the box on the right of the warning panel?   *(1 mark)*
   (b) What is antifreeze used for?   *(1 mark)*

2   The code number 2XE, for chlorine, tells the emergency services how to deal with an accident.
   (a) Why do you think the emergency services need this information?   *(1 mark)*
   (b) The code X, for chlorine, means that it should not be washed down a drain. Why is this good advice for accidents involving large amounts of chlorine?
                                                            (2 marks)
   (c) What sort of protective clothing should the emergency services wear when dealing with a chlorine tanker accident?   *(1 mark)*
   (d) Explain why a chlorine tanker carries the code E.
                                                            (1 mark)

3   Chlorine is obviously a somewhat dangerous chemical to move around on the roads.
   (a) From what raw material is chlorine made?   *(1 mark)*
   (b) Give three large-scale uses for chlorine.   *(3 marks)*
   (c) Why does chlorine need to be transported around?
                                                            (1 mark)

▶ 31 THE HAZCHEM CODE (B)

Petrol tankers are a common sight on the roads. The tanker in this photograph is being cleaned.

1 Explain the meaning of each of the three symbols in the warning panel on this petrol tanker. Say why each symbol is necessary on a petrol tanker. *(6 marks)*

2 Compare the two Hazchem warning panels for sulphuric and hydrochloric acids.

(a) In what way(s) do the emergency procedures suggested for the two acids resemble each other? Why? *(3 marks)*

(b) Explain why hydrochloric acid carries the code R, whereas sulphuric acid is code P. *(1 mark)*

3 Suppose you had a tanker containing molten sodium (sodium melts at 98 °C). What Hazchem Code symbols would you suggest? Explain the reasons for your choice. *(5 marks)*

▶ 32 AIR POLLUTION

This photograph shows an old church in the centre of London.
An overflowing gutter has washed clean part of the wall.

1   What is the main chemical pollutant which blackens the walls of town churches like this one?   *(1 mark)*

2   Explain how this pollutant gets into the air.   *(2 marks)*

3   The following table shows the amount of this pollutant, during the summer and winter months, as measured by Westminster City Council at a site close to the church.

Year	Summer concentration /μg m^{-3}	Winter concentration /μg m^{-3}
1965	36	103
1966	61	80
1967	37	65
1968	30	76
1969	26	64
1970	28	58
1971	26	57
1972	29	48
1973	25	50
1974	32	46
1975	20	36
1976	—	45
1977	21	31
1978	15	23
1979	17	33
1980	16	23
1981	12	16

The data show the average concentration of pollutant in micrograms per cubic metre, during the summer (April to September) and winter months. No figure is available for summer, 1976.

Plot, on the same set of axes, two graphs showing the year (along the bottom) and the seasonal concentrations of pollutant. (You may find a convenient scale is 1 cm = 1 year, and 1 cm = 10 μg m^{-3}).   *(5 marks)*

4   Explain why there is a difference between the summer and winter figures.   *(2 marks)*

5   Explain why the amount of pollutant has changed over the years, and why, in recent years, the summer and winter concentrations have become almost equal.   *(2 marks)*

Disaster struck the people who lived around Lake Nios, in the West African state of Cameroon. Read the newspaper report which appeared at the time.

International aid for Cameroon after second disaster strikes

Volcanic gas kills 1 500 villagers

A gas bubble disaster which has killed up to 1 500 people, believed to have been overwhelmed and 'drowned' by carbon dioxide released from a volcanic crater lake in Cameroon, will prompt an international aid effort today.

The gas rolled over a six square-mile area around Lake Nios, north-west Cameroon, catching villagers unaware and giving them no chance to escape.

The disaster is the second of its kind to strike the West African republic in almost exactly two years. The first, which claimed 35 lives in August, 1984, happened in a remote area and was regarded by experts as a baffling 'quirk of nature' which caused little alarm.

'One-off is nothing. But two in two years becomes vastly more frightening,' a British scientist who has studied the volcanic region of Cameroon said last night.

President Paul Biya, of Cameroon, said last night that at least 1 200 people had died and that another 300 were receiving medical treatment after the gas escape, which came at night while villagers were asleep. Travellers from the area gave higher estimates to the toll.

Rescue teams were trekking into the area carrying oxygen cylinders by back pack to replenish exhausted supplies. A doctor in the capital, Yaounde, said that the victims were suffering burning pains in the eyes and nose, coughing and signs of asphyxiation similar to strangulation. It was like being gased by a kitchen stove, he said.

'The ideal treatment is to give victims pure oxygen, but we don't have any up there.' Casualties appeared to have been affected by a mixture of gases, including hydrogen and sulphur. Hydrogen sulphide is commonly released in volcanic areas but vulcanologists agreed yesterday that it was unlikely to be responsible for the mass deaths.

It has a strong rotten eggs smell which would warn of its release, and it is also lighter than air and would disperse rapidly. British experts believe that a carbon dioxide release is a more likely cause.

Dr Godfrey Fitton, a lecturer in geology at Edinburgh University, has first-hand knowledge of the volcanic area which lies along the Cameroon–Nigeria border, where Mount Cameroon (4 070 metres), the highest peak in West Africa, has had four lava outbursts this century.

He believes that one possible explanation for the gas escape may be heavy rainfall—the rainy season covers August—disturbing the waters of the lake where the gas has been trapped, and triggering its release.

The gas comes from vertical pipes, filled with rubble, which have been fed from an extinct volcano.

The gas could either be trapped by sediment in the lake bottom or held in the water in the depths of the lake.

'These lakes are very deep and the bottom waters become saturated with carbon dioxide, forming a sort of soda water at the bottom. You get a dramatic overturn and this bottom water comes up to the top. Heavy rainfall could be the thing which triggers it. This is pure speculation.

'People being suffocated by carbon dioxide is not an uncommon phenomenon in volcanic areas. Carbon dioxide is the most common volcanic gas and any volcano in its last gasp is likely to be putting out carbon dioxide.'

'It would be like a thick blanket that would cover the villages,' a US expert, Mr William Nelson, said yesterday. 'Imagine a sheet of dense gases moving over the villages. The people wouldn't have had enough time to get away.'

Guardian, 26 August 1986
(by Andrew Moncur)

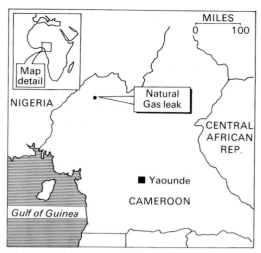

The area of the disaster

1 Why would the people be 'drowned' by carbon dioxide?
(1 mark)

2 'The ideal treatment is to give victims pure oxygen...' Why is pure oxygen the best treatment? *(1 mark)*

3 What does the newspaper mean when it says the 'waters become saturated with carbon dioxide'? *(1 mark)*

4 'Casualties appeared to have been affected by a mixture of gases, including hydrogen and sulphur. Hydrogen sulphide is commonly released...'

   (a) Do you think it likely that you would get sulphur gas? Explain your reasoning. *(2 marks)*

   (b) 'It would be like a thick blanket that would cover the villages...' Do you think it likely that this would contain hydrogen gas? Explain your reasoning. *(2 marks)*

   (c) 'Hydrogen sulphide is commonly released...' Use the periodic table at the end of the book to give the name of another compound of hydrogen which you would expect to be similar to hydrogen sulphide in its properties. Explain why you have chosen this compound. *(2 marks)*

   (d) What would you expect the formula of hydrogen sulphide to be? *(1 mark)*

   (e) Hydrogen sulphide is a poisonous gas. Why do you think that the newspaper report does not suggest anybody was poisoned? *(1 mark)*

Stain salts can be added to washing powders to improve their ability to remove stains.

Contains
no phosphate
or chlorine bleach
Suitable for all washable
fabrics including
colourfast items

Original
StainSalts
BY STAIN DEVILS

Even today's washing powders cannot completely remove stubborn stains such as vegetable, grass, red wine, blood, coffee, tea, fruit, spice and really ingrained dirt. But now the new scientific formula of StainSalts actually boosts the power of your powder to remove even the most stubborn stains during the wash.

Simply add a few spoons of StainSalts to the main cycle of the wash. The active oxygen ingredients will go to work breaking down the stains and ingrained dirt, leaving your clothes and fabrics stain-free and cleaner than you ever thought possible.

How much to use for Full Loads	30°C - 40°C	60 g (8 heaped teaspoons)
	60°C	50 g (7 heaped teaspoons)
	95°C	40 g (6 heaped teaspoons)

Add to the washing powder for the main wash cycle.

· The higher the temperature the better the result, but follow the washing instructions on the garment label. For heavily soiled items (eg work clothes or nappies) you can add 60 g (8 teaspoons) of StainSalts to a bucket of hot water and leave to soak. Alternatively, add it to the pre-wash container in your machine.
· Do not soak wool, leather, silk, non-colourfast or flame resistant articles
· StainSalts are suitable for use with all washing powders and liquid detergents
· Will not harm textiles or your washing machine

STAIN SALTS - Contains Sodium Percarbonate
Irritating to eyes, respiratory system and skin
Keep out of reach of children
Keep away from heat
Avoid contact with skin and eyes
In case of contact with eyes, rinse immediately with plenty of water and seek medical advice
If swallowed seek medical advice immediately and show this container or label

IRRITANT.
DDD Ltd
Watford, Herts

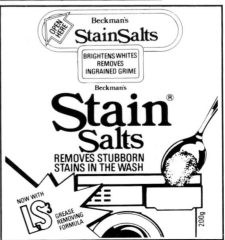

OPEN HERE
Beckman's
StainSalts

BRIGHTENS WHITES
REMOVES
INGRAINED GRIME

Beckman's
Stain®
Salts
REMOVES STUBBORN
STAINS IN THE WASH

NOW WITH
LS³
GREASE
REMOVING
FORMULA

200g

▶ 34 STAIN SALTS (A)

1 By what *type* of reaction do you think the stain salts break down the stains? *(1 mark)*

2 Suggest a reason why 60 g of stain salts are needed at 30–40 °C, but only 50 g at 60 °C, and 40 g at 95 °C. *(2 marks)*

3 This product's label claims that it is better than ordinary washing powders at removing stains such as grass, wine, etc. How would you test whether this claim is true? Describe carefully the investigations you would carry out, and how you would make sure the tests were fair. *(5 marks)*

▶ 35 STAIN SALTS (B)

Stain salts contain sodium percarbonate. The prefix *per* in the name of a compound suggests that it is rich in oxygen.

1 Many compounds which are rich in oxygen will release oxygen gas if warmed gently.
- **(a)** Draw a labelled diagram of the apparatus you would use to see if stain salts release a gas on heating. *(2 marks)*
- **(b)** How would you test any such gas released to see if it was, in fact, oxygen? *(2 marks)*

2 Adding acid to carbonates will normally give carbon dioxide.
- **(a)** How can you test for the presence of carbon dioxide? *(1 mark)*
- **(b)** What would happen if you carried out the 'oxygen test' on carbon dioxide? *(1 mark)*

3 If you added acid to sodium percarbonate, you might expect to get a mixture of both oxygen and carbon dioxide. Draw a labelled diagram of the apparatus you would use to test this idea. Explain carefully how you would use your apparatus to check whether one or both of these gases were present. *(4 marks)*

4 What test would you carry out to confirm that stain salts contain a compound of sodium? *(2 marks)*

The following information about fire extinguishers comes from the catalogue of a large supplier.

Fire Protection Equipment
EXTINGUISHERS

Water CO_2 extinguishers are for use on Class A fires involving carbonaceous materials such as paper, wood and textiles, etc. Easily operated and re-charged. All extinguishers are supplied with hoses but fixed nozzle versions can be obtained if required.

Foam type extinguishers are suitable for use on Class B fires involving flammable liquids such as paint, oil, petrol, etc. They can also be used on some Class A fires involving paper, wood, textiles, etc., but they must not be used on live electrical equipment. The extinguishers generate foam with a minimum expansion ratio of 8:1 thus 16 gallons of foam are produced by the 2 gallon model. The foam forms a blanket over the burning liquid and seals it from the oxygen in the air.

CO_2 extinguishers are suitable for use on Class B fires involving flammable liquids such as oil, petrol and paint etc. and on Class C fires involving live electrical equipment. CO_2 is a non-conductor of electricity. It is clean and non-corrosive and is ideal for use on delicate mechanical and electrical equipment. CO_2 is heavier than air and will penetrate otherwise inaccessible areas.

Dry powder extinguishers are for use on Class B fires involving liquids such as oil, petrol, paint, etc. and on Class C fires involving gases and live electrical equipment. These cartridge operated extinguishers are supplied fully charged and ready for use. They are quickly re-charged using a standard refill pack, containing powder, cartridge and 'FULL' plug. The powerful stream of powder acts as a heat shield whilst the fire is extinguished. The dry powder used is a non-conductor of electricity, is non-toxic, non-abrasive and is unaffected by normal changes in temperature.

The most popular extinguishers are stocked at the depot, but all types and sizes of fire fighting equipment are available via direct supply. The Fire Brigade will advise on selection and placement of 'First Aid' fire fighting equipment.

1   Copy this table, and use the information given to fill in the gaps.

Type of fire extinguisher	Suitable for use on fires involving:	One advantage of this type of extinguisher
Water CO_2		
Foam		
CO_2		
Dry powder		

(8 marks)

2   **(a)** Which two types of fire extinguisher can be used on electrical fires? *(2 marks)*

    (b) Why are the other types of extinguisher *not* suitable for electrical fires? *(2 marks)*

3   A foam extinguisher forms a blanket over a burning liquid. Why does this put the fire out? *(1 mark)*

4   **(a)** What sorts of materials are burning in class A fires? *(1 mark)*

    (b) What sorts of materials are burning in class B fires? *(1 mark)*

    (c) What problems might arise if you tried to use a water CO_2 extinguisher on a class B fire? *(1 mark)*

▶ 37 HUNGARIAN CHEMISTRY

It's not very likely that you can understand Hungarian, but the symbols of chemistry form an international language. This is one item from a Hungarian book of chemistry questions.

> **216.** Az ammónia oxidációs folyamatát az alábbi egyenlet fejezi ki:
>
> $$4NH_3 + 5O_2 = 4NO + 6H_2O \quad Q = -226{,}5\,kJ/mól$$
>
> Az egyenletekben szereplő vegyületek közül a NO képződéshője pozitív, az NH_3 és a víz képződéshője negatív. Ennek ismeretében magyarázzuk meg, miért kell a reakciót nagy reakciósebességgel lejátszatni, majd a reakciótermékeket gyorsan lehűteni?

1   Describe in your own words the chemical reaction which is being considered in this question. *(3 marks)*

2   In this reaction, what is being oxidized? To what is it oxidized? *(2 marks)*

3   **(a)** This reaction is one step in an important manufacturing process. What is being manufactured? *(1 mark)*

    (b) Why is it so important to manufacture this product? *(2 marks)*

4   How does the Hungarian author indicate that this reaction is exothermic? *(1 mark)*

These are parts of a leaflet called *Help yourself to gas safety*, produced by the public relations department of British Gas.

8 | Ventilation

Gas appliances must breathe – in and out, just like people. While burning they need to breathe in fresh air, so that burning of the gas takes place safely and efficiently. This fresh air supply is often provided by ventilators such as those shown here. Never block them.

9 | Chimneys and flues

Many gas appliances need a chimney or flue to make sure they can breathe out after burning the gas and fresh air. This chimney makes sure that the fumes from the appliance are not mixed with the fresh air you need to breathe. Thus it is most important to make sure the chimney is swept to see it is clear of anything which could block it – bird's nests, broken bricks or soot. **This must be done thoroughly before any appliance is fitted to the chimney.**

Broken bricks, mortar or soot can create danger by falling down the chimney and blocking it behind the fire.

If chimneys or flues do become blocked, the fumes will spill into the room, polluting the air you need to breathe with deadly carbon monoxide – a colourless, odourless, highly poisonous gas.

Signs of this happening are staining, sooting or discoloration round a gas fire (like the one below) or a water heater   A yellow or orange flame in an appliance may also be an indication.

Unfortunately, the symptoms of carbon monoxide poisoning are vague, and can be confused with symptoms produced by many other causes – even a cold or influenza, for instance. Unexplained headaches, sickness, chronic tiredness, or muscular weakness are other possible signs. If you or others suffer from such symptoms after being in a room where a fuel burning appliance is in use, it is wise to see your doctor, and to call in an expert to check the appliance. At the first sign of any of these symptoms, stop using the appliance and call gas service. To ignore them could be dangerous.

Many new models of appliances have a special built-in system, which seals both ventilation and flueing from the atmosphere of the room. These take fresh air directly from, and discharge their fumes directly to, the outside of the house. Known as 'balanced flue' or 'room sealed' such appliances must be fitted to an outside wall. They are the best choice wherever they can be fitted.

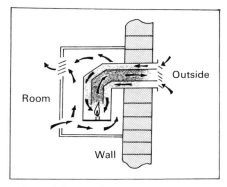

Balanced flue appliance

▶ 38   GAS SAFETY (A)

1   What is the chemical name of the main substance present in natural gas?   *(1 mark)*

2   **(a)** 'Gas appliances must breathe in and out.' What do they breathe in?   *(1 mark)*
   (b) What do they breathe out, if working safely?   *(1 mark)*
   (c) What gas might they breathe out if not working safely?   *(1 mark)*
   (d) Why would the formation of this gas be a problem?   *(1 mark)*

3   Give two different ways by which you might recognize if a gas appliance is not working safely.   *(2 marks)*

4   What is the most likely cause of a gas appliance not working safely?   *(1 mark)*

5   Why do gas appliances often need a flue or chimney?   *(1 mark)*

6   Explain what is meant by a 'balanced flue'.   *(1 mark)*

▶ 39   GAS SAFETY (B)

Look at the seven simple safety rules about water heaters and the extracts from the British Gas safety leaflet on pages 46–47.

/10/ Water heaters

Water heaters need plenty of fresh air too. For a number of years it has been the law that only balanced flue models may be fitted in bathrooms. However, there are many older types with ordinary flues still giving good service, but they do so only when some simple safety rules are followed:

● Make sure your bathroom is well ventilated and the flue system above the water heater is not broken or damaged.

● Open the bathroom window or door while drawing off hot water.

● Turn off the gas water heater **before** you get into the bath.

● To be doubly safe, don't run more hot water while you're in the bath.

● Keep bathroom ventilators free from obstruction.

● Have the water heater serviced regularly – at least once a year.

● With unflued instantaneous sink water heaters, make sure you do not run the heater continuously for more than five minutes. Such heaters are not designed for filling baths or washing machines, or for showers. These heaters too should be serviced at least once a year. You will find clear safety instructions on every new instantaneous gas water heater.

The sooty marks on this water heater indicate danger.

Either **(a)** Write an article for a newspaper, explaining why each of these rules is necessary.

or   **(b)** Draw or paint a poster to remind people about the safety rules. (You could imagine that it was going to be stuck on to the water heater, as a permanent reminder.)

or   **(c)** Write a short play, which would show people why the safety rules are necessary.   *(10 marks)*

▶ 40   GAS SAFETY (C)

Look at the extracts from the British Gas safety leaflet on pages 46–48. These three equations represent possible reactions when gas burns:

$$CH_4 + 2O_2 \longrightarrow CO_2 + 2H_2O \quad \mathbf{X}$$

$$2CH_4 + 3O_2 \longrightarrow 2CO + 4H_2O \quad \mathbf{Y}$$

$$CH_4 + O_2 \longrightarrow C + 2H_2O \quad \mathbf{Z}$$

1   Which of the reactions **X**, **Y** and **Z** are exothermic and which endothermic? Why do you say so?   *(2 marks)*

2   Copy down equation **X**, and write-in the symbols of state [(g), (l), (s), (aq)] assuming room temperature.   *(2 marks)*

3   If a pan of cold water is placed on a gas ring, condensation is often seen on the outside of the pan soon after lighting the gas. Suggest why.   *(1 mark)*

4   In equation **X**, what is oxidized and what is reduced?   *(2 marks)*

5   Which one of the equations **X**, **Y**, or **Z** represents the safe burning of gas?   *(1 mark)*

6   Which one of the reactions shown in equations **X**, **Y** and **Z** would result in the formation of soot?   *(1 mark)*

7   Which one of the reactions shown in equations **X**, **Y** and **Z** would produce a poisonous gas?   *(1 mark)*

8   If you started off with 1 litre of gas, which of the reactions shown in equations **X**, **Y** and **Z** would use most air? Explain how you arrive at your answer.   *(2 marks)*

This newspaper cutting reports an accident which happened in a sulphuric acid factory in India.

DELHI PANIC AS GAS LEAK INJURES 250

Gas leaking from a chemical factory injured more than 250 people yesterday, just one day after the first anniversary of the Bhopal disaster which killed 2 500.

Choking white fumes engulfed an area where about 200 000 people live and work in the bustling bazaar districts of the capital's old walled city. Earlier this year, a safety expert urged the Government to shut down the plant, which produces sulphuric acid.

The leak, which sent thousands of people fleeing from their homes, shops and offices in north and west Delhi, occurred after a 40-ton tank containing olium, a highly acidic gas, collapsed inside the factory.

The gas, which formed a thick smog over several square miles, left people retching and coughing violently as it attacked their throats and lungs. Others were struck temporarily blind and many complained of a burning sensation in their eyes hours after the leak.

No deaths were reported, but more than 250 people were admitted to hospital. Most were released later in the day but at least 17 people were seriously ill, hospital sources said.

Police have arrested three factory officials, including its general manager, and charged them with causing injury by a negligent act.

According to a police spokesman, the tank collapsed after the olium inside it overflowed and melted down its metal stand. The olium then mixed with water in the sewage system and formed a pungent gas cloud. Several years ago, the factory was declared a health hazard.

Experts from the Central Pollution Control Board and the Council of Scientific and Industrial Research who visited the factory later, said that while the gas was highly corrosive, it was not toxic.

The gas leak a day after the first anniversary of the Bhopal gas disaster, sparked an unprecedented panic in the city. Caught by surprise, the city administration failed to stop people from leaving their houses until later in the day, although it had been established within a few hours of the leak the gas was not lethal.

The former labour commissioner, Mrs Nita Bali, warned the government after Bhopal about low safety standards at the Shriram Food and Fertilizer plant. She recommended closing the factory which stored more than 280 tons of deadly chlorine gas in densely populated areas.

Guardian, 5 December 1985
(by Ajoy Bose)

Oleum, wrongly spelt by the newspaper as olium, is sulphur trioxide, SO_3, dissolved in concentrated sulphuric acid, H_2SO_4. You could think of the formula of oleum as $H_2S_2O_7$.

Substance	Melting point/°C	Boiling point/°C
H_2SO_4	10	338
SO_3	17	45
$H_2S_2O_7$	35	

1   What is the physical state (gas/liquid/solid) of each of these three substances at room temperature and atmospheric pressure?   *(3 marks)*

2   Oleum reacts violently with water to form a mist of concentrated sulphuric acid droplets. Write a balanced chemical equation for this reaction, including symbols of state [(g), (l), (s), (aq)].   *(2 marks)*

3   Which of the warning signs would you expect on a container of oleum? What does it mean?   *(2 marks)*

4   Sulphuric acid manufacture is obviously dangerous. Why is it made on such a large scale? What is it used for that it is so important?   *(2 marks)*

5   Write a letter to the newspaper, explaining why you think the statement '... the olium inside it overflowed and melted down its metal stand ...' is not correct. What should the report have said?   *(3 marks)*

6   This accident happened in India, a Third World country. Do you think it could have happened in a developed country, such as Britain? Explain your reasons.   *(3 marks)*

A

B

C

D

E

F

G

TATE + LYLE CANE SUGAR

Quick dissolving sugar

CONTENTS
APPROX ONE LEVEL
TEASPOON

▶ 42–43   WHITE SUGAR

This packet of sugar was supplied with a cup of tea on a train.

▶ 42   WHITE SUGAR (A)

1   What do you think is likely to be different about the sugar in this packet which makes it 'quick dissolving'?   *(1 mark)*

2   How would this difference make it dissolve more quickly than ordinary sugar?   *(1 mark)*

3   How would you try to prove that this sugar was, in fact, quick dissolving? Say carefully what experiments you would do, what equipment you would use, how you would make your tests fair, and what you would expect to happen.   *(4 marks)*

▶ 43   WHITE SUGAR (B)

1   Cane sugar has the formula $C_{12}H_{22}O_{11}$. If a level teaspoon holds about 6.84 g of sugar, about how many moles are there in this packet of white sugar?   *(2 marks)*

2   If this amount of sugar is dissolved in one cup of tea, volume 200 cm³, what is the concentration of the sugar solution in mol dm⁻³ (i.e., its molarity)?   *(2 marks)*

▶ 44   POISONED WINE

Read the report about poisoned Italian wine.

1   What name is given to the process in which grape juice is turned into wine?   *(1 mark)*

2   Apart from water, the main substance you would expect to find in wine is alcohol. What is its chemical name?   *(1 mark)*

3   The poisoning of this Italian wine was due to the presence of methyl alcohol (wood alcohol). What is the modern chemical name for this substance?   *(1 mark)*

4   What percentage of methyl alcohol is legally allowed in Italian wine?   *(1 mark)*

Laced wine death toll reaches 12

A 52-year-old man died in Genoa yesterday, taking to 12 the number of people known to have been killed in the past two weeks by adulterated Italian wine. Twelve more are in hospital in northern Italy after drinking the wine, and some of them are expected to be left blind by the methyl (or wood) alcohol added to the wine either by producers or bottlers.

Magistrates have arrested two wholesalers and warned some traders they could face prosecution. More than 180 000 gallons of wine have been confiscated from several north Italian bottling plants.

Doctors said that Mr Fermino Minari came to the hospital's eye department last week saying he had gone blind after drinking suspect wine. He suddenly collapsed, went into a coma and died of a heart attack.

Significant traces of methyl alcohol, or methanol, were found in his blood and urine, the hospital said.

Wine experts said the illegal addition of methyl alcohol to wine to increase its potency could have been taking place for years. But, they say, it reached fatal proportions this year because of the unusually high methyl alcohol content naturally present in last year's vintage.

Methyl alcohol is a natural product of grape pressing which derives from the stems of the fruit. A level of 0.03 per cent is legally allowed to be added to wine. But samples of the lethal wine, discovered two weeks ago after the first deaths were reported, contained as much as 3 per cent.

Piedmont authorities said that the production of wood alcohol had been subject to a modest tax until 1968, and its use was also monitored. Now it is tax free and the control has gone. Also, they say, even in major wine-growing areas such as Asti, where the wine is carefully certified, there are not enough staff to carry out the complicated test for the methyl content.

Some of the so-called 'Piedmont' wines—generally considered to be among Italy's finest—have been mixed with a cheaper wine imported from Apulia, in the heel of the Italian boot. It is possible that methyl could have been added there to raise the alcohol content. Apulia produces its own fine wines, and even exports some of its produce to France in tankers.

The lethal wine sold in northern Italy was sold in northern Italian supermarkets and came in metal capped bottles.

Guardian, 2 April 1986
(by George Armstrong)

5 What percentage of methyl alcohol was actually found in this Italian wine? *(1 mark)*

6 What are the main effects of drinking methyl alcohol? *(2 marks)*

7 Which of the symbols on page 51 would you expect to find on a bottle of pure methyl alcohol? Explain why. *(2 marks)*

8 Here is some information about the chemicals present in this wine:

Substance	Melting point/°C	Boiling point/°C	Solubility
Methyl alcohol	−94	65	*These three mix in all proportions*
Alcohol	−117	79	
Water	0	100	

(a) Draw a labelled diagram of the apparatus you would use to try to obtain some pure methyl alcohol from the wine. *(3 marks)*

(b) How would you know whether the methyl alcohol you had obtained was pure? *(1 mark)*

(c) What name is given to the process carried out in the apparatus you have just drawn? *(1 mark)*

▶ 45 AEROSOL FIREBALL

Read this story of an horrific accident involving aerosol cans.

FIREBALL HORROR OF AEROSOL CAN BLAST

Housewife is human torch

A HOUSEWIFE was engulfed in a fireball when she tried to separate two bargain-offer cans of hairspray.

Mrs Lydia Owen accidentally punctured one aerosol can with a knife as she cut the tape binding them together.

A jet of butane gas shot into her living room fire and ignited.

The can immediately exploded into a fireball, wrecking the room and covering Lydia, 67, in flames.

Fumes

But, despite 30 per cent burns, she helped her 68-year-old bed-ridden husband, Fred, to safety from their shattered home in Walsall, West Midlands.

Lydia was in 'a serious condition' in hospital last night.

Fred was recovering from the effects of choking fumes.

A fire officer said: 'She was a very brave woman. She must have been in great pain, but still got her husband out of the house.'

Daily Mirror, 30 December 1985

1 Which of the hazard warning symbols would you expect to find on this aerosol can? *(1 mark)*

2 As a result of this accident, write a suitable warning message to go on this type of can. *(1 mark)*

3 Butane is used in spray cans as both a *solvent* for the hair lacquer and as a *propellant*. Explain the meaning of the words solvent and propellant as used here. *(2 marks)*

4 The boiling point of butane is $-1\,^\circ\text{C}$, and its melting point is $-138\,^\circ\text{C}$.
    (a) Would you normally expect butane to be a gas, a liquid or a solid at room temperature? *(1 mark)*
    (b) Explain why butane is present as a liquid in aerosol cans. *(1 mark)*

5 Butane is sometimes deliberately used as a fuel.
    (a) Give an example of where it is used as a fuel. *(1 mark)*
    (b) Butane has the formula C_4H_{10}. What would you expect to form when it burns? *(2 marks)*
    (c) Write a balanced chemical equation for the burning of butane. *(2 marks)*

6 Freons (fluorochlorocarbons such as CF_2Cl_2) are sometimes used in place of butane in aerosol cans. They do not burn, but there is a fear that they may damage the layer of ozone in the Earth's upper atmosphere. This layer protects human beings from the harmful effects of ultraviolet radiation. Write a letter to the newspaper, arguing *for* or *against* the continued use of butane in aerosol cans. *(4 marks)*

A

B

C

D

E

F

G

▶ 46 MURIATIC ACID

The following extracts are taken from *The Chemical Catechism* by Samuel Parkes, a chemistry book published in 1808.

What method is made use of to collect and preserve the muriatic acid?

Muriatic acid is distilled from sea salt by means of sulphuric acid, and collected in appropriate receivers, where it is condensed in water, for which it has a powerful affinity.

What are the properties of muriatic acid?

This acid in the gaseous state is invisible like air; has a pungent suffocating smell; and is not decomposable by art. With water it forms the liquid muriatic acid, which preserves the smell of the gas, and gives out white fumes when exposed to the atmosphere. This acid is much employed in the arts, and in chemical laboratories. With various bases it forms the salts called *muriates*.

What is the oxygenized muriatic acid?

The oxygenized muriatic acid is formed with muriatic acid and oxygen.† It is known in the gaseous state, and in combination with water: in the latter form it is commonly used in the arts.

What are the properties of oxygenized muriatic acid?

The oxygenized muriatic acid gas is so suffocating, that it cannot be breathed without great injury; yet it will support combustion. This acid discharges vegetable colours; it oxidizes all the metals and is the only acid that will dissolve gold and platina. With various bases it forms salts, called hyperoxygenized muriates.

†Muriatic acid has a great affinity for oxygen. When fully oxygenized it seems to have lost several of its acid properties, as it is even incapable of expelling carbonic acid from alkalies or lime, except in its nascent state. If oxygenized muriatic acid be exposed to light, the light combines with part of the oxygen, and the oxygenized muriatic acid is then converted into common muriatic acid.

The effect of giving a dose of oxygen to this acid is quite the reverse of the acid of sulphur, it being rendered more volatile thereby, and of a very penetrating smell; whereas the addition of oxygen to sulphurous acid gives it more density, and renders it quite inodorous. The combination of oxygen gives a greenish yellow colour to this gas. Common muriatic acid gas is invisible.

Oxygenized muriatic acid gas may be obtained for chemical experiments by the following method: Put into a retort a little black oxide of manganese in powder; and pour upon this double its weight of strong muriatic acid, connect the retort with the pneumatic trough, and receive the gas over water. When the ascension of the gas slackens, apply the heat of a lamp, and it will be disengaged in abundance.

1 **(a)** What is the modern chemical name for sea salt?

(1 mark)

(b) What gas would you expect to get if you added sulphuric acid to sea salt? (Give its modern name.)

(1 mark)

(c) What do you think is the modern name for muriatic acid? *(1 mark)*

2 **(a)** 'Oxygenized muriatic acid' is said to be a greenish-yellow colour. What greenish-yellow-coloured gases do you know? *(1 mark)*

(b) Does the greenish-yellow gas that you know contain oxygen? *(1 mark)*

(c) If you made the greenish-yellow gas from muriatic acid, we would not, in modern terminology, say that the muriatic acid had been 'oxygenized'. What would we say instead? *(1 mark)*

3 Look at the description of how 'oxygenized muriatic acid' may be obtained. Draw a labelled diagram showing how you would make 'oxygenized muriatic acid' using equipment likely to be found in a school laboratory. *(3 marks)*

Toxic gas drives pupils out of classrooms

NEARLY 600 boys will assemble outside their school in Essex with their satchels, briefcases and boxes of textbooks just before 9 am tomorrow. Instead of going in to begin their lessons, they will board a fleet of buses that will take them to study in spare rooms at four schools nearby.

They cannot use their own school because a poisonous gas, produced by a heat-insulating material, has driven them out of their classrooms. The toxic gas has caused an epidemic of vomiting, headaches, sore throats, chest pains and streaming eyes among pupils and teachers.

The St Thomas More boys' secondary school at Westcliff-on-Sea has now been closed, for the third time in two months, while experts try to solve the problem. The pupils meanwhile, are beginning their third week of 'bussing' to alternative accommodation.

The affair has called into serious question the safety of the heat insulating material, called urea-formaldehyde foam (UF foam), which gives off the irritant gas when it is pumped into the cavity walls of houses and other buildings and sets hard. This use of UF foam has been banned in the US and Canada because of fears about its safety.

As well as being widely used in public buildings to cut fuel bills, UF foam has been installed in $1\frac{1}{4}$ million private houses in Britain. Contractors are now injecting foam into the cavity walls of about 100 000 homes a year — and cases of private householders suffering from the ill-effects of toxic formaldehyde gas are mounting.

There are growing fears that the standard code of practice, which contractors must follow when installing the foam, is inadequate.

The parents of children at St Thomas More school are angry about what has happened. As well as being concerned about their children's health, they are worried about the disruption to their studies, particularly in an exam term.

'We want the cavity foam removed immediately,' said Peter Roper, who is chairman of the school's parents' association. 'Whatever remedial works are carried out, we will never be completely certain that our children's health will not be affected in the long term.'

Roper's son Simon suffers with repeated attacks of bronchitis. 'He came home one day with streaming eyes,' his father said. 'I was on the verge of getting the doctor to put him on a course of antibiotics when we found out about the foam.'

The parents have hardly been reassured by recent government pronouncements on the subject. Junior environment minister Sir George Young informed the Commons a week ago that studies so far of people exposed to formaldehyde had not found any evidence that the gas causes cancer or lung damage.

British medical opinion is sceptical about the possible cancer-causing effects. But in America, a panel of scientists convened by the Consumer Product Safety Commission two years ago concluded that 'it is prudent to regard formaldehyde as posing a carcinogenic risk to humans.'

Signs of trouble began at St Thomas More school soon after the UF foam was pumped into the wall cavities just before Easter. When pupils and staff reported sick, the buildings were closed while the Health and Safety Executive tested for gas.

The inspectors found concentrations of up to 0.6 parts per million (ppm)—well below the executive's recommended maximum exposure level of 2 ppm, but more than enough to cause the distressing symptoms.

Early attempts to solve the problem failed and the school closed again. Essex county council, which partly funds the church school and ordered the insulation work as part of its energy conservation programme, called in an independent technical expert, Dr David Barrett.

'The problem was caused by gaps under the window sills which allow air to be blown into the cavity, pushing formaldehyde gas through openings in the inner leaf of the wall and into the classroom,' Barrett explained. He has proposed sealing the gaps and blowing ammonia through the cavities in an attempt to neutralize the formaldehyde.

Dr Barrett, who still sits on the relevant British Standards committee, concedes that a review of BS 5618 is long overdue. Its major shortcoming is that it does not stress the importance of having a continuous, gas-tight inner leaf or skin to a cavity wall before the foam is pumped in.

The Sunday Times, 16 May 1982

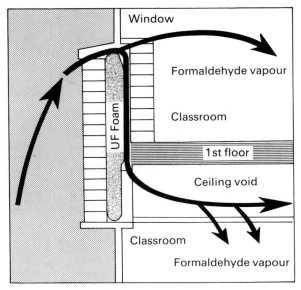

How the gas entered the classrooms

1　**(a)** Why is it usually considered a good idea to put an insulating material in the cavities between walls?
(2 marks)

　(b) Why was UF foam chosen as a suitable material to put in the cavities between walls?　*(2 marks)*

2　UF Foam is a polymer. It can be formed where it is needed—in the gaps between walls—by mixing two monomers with a suitable catalyst.

　(a) Suggest the names of the two monomers from which UF foam is made.　*(2 marks)*

　(b) Why is a catalyst necessary?　*(1 mark)*

　(c) Suggest why it is an advantage to be able to make the polymer in the cavities, where it is needed.　*(1 mark)*

　(d) With the help of diagrams, explain what is meant by a polymer.　*(2 marks)*

3　UF foam is a solid, but formaldehyde is a gas.

　(a) Which would have the higher melting point?　*(1 mark)*

　(b) Explain the reasons for your answer to **(a)**.　*(1 mark)*

4　It is proposed to solve the problem described in this newspaper article by blowing ammonia gas through the wall cavities to neutralize the formaldehyde.

　(a) What does the term 'neutralize' mean?　*(1 mark)*

　(b) What does this suggest about the properties of formaldehyde?　*(1 mark)*

▶ 48 ICE CREAM

Compare these labels from Lyons Maid Chocolate and Banana ice cream and Wall's Cornetto ice cream cones. (A list of E-numbers is given at the end of the book.)

Soft Scoop

Chocolate & Banana Flavour

CHOCOLATE & BANANA FLAVOUR

ICE CREAMS
(CONTAIN NON-MILK FAT)

2 litre

INGREDIENTS: Skimmed milk, sugar, vegetable fat, glucose syrup, glycerine, whey powder, fat reduced cocoa, emulsifier (E471), stabilisers (E412, E407), colours (E102, E110, E122, E142), flavouring, salt

Lyons Maid Limited, Glacier House, Brook Green, London W6 7BT

Wall's

Cornetto™
4 STRAWBERRY CONES

INGREDIENTS: SKIMMED MILK, SUGAR, VEGETABLE FAT, STRAWBERRY PUREE, FLOUR, GLUCOSE SYRUP, WHEY SOLIDS, FAT REDUCED COCOA, EMULSIFIERS (LECITHIN, E471), CITRIC ACID, STABILISERS (CARRAGEENAN, CAROB GUM, GUAR GUM), COLOURS (ANNATTO, E161 (g), BETANIN), SALT, FLAVOURING.
4 x 110 ml

WALL'S ICE CREAM LTD STATION AVENUE WALTON-ON-THAMES SURREY ENGLAND

1 Draw up a table to compare the ingredients in the two ice creams. The table has been started to help you.

Ingredient	Lyons Maid Chocolate and Banana	Wall's Cornetto
Skimmed milk	✓	✓

(3 marks)

2 **(a)** Give the name(s) (*not* just the E-numbers) of any colourings present in Lyons Maid Chocolate and Banana which are not present in Wall's Cornetto.
(1 mark)

(b) Give the name(s) of any colourings present in Wall's Cornetto which are not present in Lyons Maid Chocolate and Banana. *(1 mark)*

(c) Some countries ban the use of the colour E102. Could either, or both, of these ice creams be sold in such countries? *(1 mark)*

3 **(a)** Predict a likely pH for Wall's Cornetto. How did you arrive at your prediction? *(2 marks)*

(b) Would you expect Lyons Maid Chocolate and Banana to have a similar pH? Give a reason for your answer.
(2 marks)

4 How would you attempt to see if Lyons Maid Chocolate and Banana contains some water? *(2 marks)*

5 Various foods are mixed with water, and then tested as shown in the following table. Copy out the table and fill in the gaps. *(7 marks)*

Test	Sucrose (cane sugar)	Glucose	Starch	Lyons Maid Chocolate and Banana	Wall's Cornetto
Warm with Benedict's Solution	No change	Blue solution gives orange precipitate	?	?	?
Add iodine solution	No change	?	Blue-black colour	?	?
Add silver nitrate solution	No change	No change	No change	?	White precipitate

6 What reaction causes the white precipitate when silver nitrate solution is added to Wall's Cornetto cones? *(1 mark)*

▶ 49 COAL FIRES

This is part of an advertisement for coal fires, which appeared in the *Observer*.

If you share the inclination, along with countless other people these days, to get back to the real things in life, you could start by opening up your fireplace, and preparing a coal fire in the grate.

Coal is as old as the hills, and just as natural.

And it's been going every bit as long as wheatgerm, organic cabbages or juice straight from the fruit.

What's more, there's at least 300 years'

> NO ADDITIVES
> NO PRESERVATIVES
> NO ARTIFICIAL COLOURING
> BEST BEFORE SEPT 2286

worth of coal still under the ground in Britain.

Nothing beats a coal fire to come home to, especially on a real winter's day, when there's a chill in the wind, and more than a touch of frost on the trees outside.

Happily, an increasing number of people are rediscovering the magic of a real fire.

British housecoal and its smokeless coal cousins are very much the fuels in fashion.

For further information about real fires, or real fire appliances, contact your Approved Coal Merchant, Freefone Real Fires, or write to Solid Fuel Advisory Service, Freepost, Sunderland SR9 9AD. (No stamp required.)

Real fires start with British Coal.

---

1 'Coal is as old as the hills, and just as natural'. Is this true? How did coal form? *(3 marks)*

2 **(a)** '...there's at least 300 years' worth of coal still under the ground in Britain'. What is assumed in this statement? *(1 mark)*

(b) How does this figure of 300 years for coal compare with figures for North Sea oil and gas? *(2 marks)*

3 Coal fires are less popular than they used to be. One reason for this is the pollution that they can cause.

(a) Give the names of *two* pollutants which can result from burning coal, and explain carefully how each is formed. *(4 marks)*

(b) Give an account of some of the problems which may be caused by these pollutants. *(4 marks)*

4 The advertisement refers to 'housecoal' and 'smokeless coal'. Devise an experiment to measure which of these two fuels gives the most heat. Say what equipment you would use, how you would use it, what you would measure, and how you would interpret your results. *(4 marks)*

▶ 50–55 SWIMMING POOLS

These questions are all concerned with extracts from a manual of instructions for caretakers and others operating swimming pools of various sorts in schools.

Chlorine Gas Installations

These notes apply only to schools which use chlorine gas from cylinders as the method of disinfection of the swimming pool water.

Chlorine gas is provided in yellow 33 kg cylinders. These cylinders contain liquid chlorine under pressure, which becomes a gas when the cylinder valve is opened and the pressure reduces.

Chlorine gas is a lung irritant and at high concentrations is toxic and lethal, so great care is needed when using it.

The use of chlorine gas is normally confined to the larger swimming pools. When applied correctly, the use of chlorine gas causes the pH of the pool water to fall (i.e., the water becomes more acid) and consequently soda ash (sodium carbonate) is added to raise the pH value and enable the pH of the water to be maintained between the recommended limits of 7.6–8.0.

Soda ash is provided in 50 kg paper sacks. The powder may irritate the skin and care must be taken when handling the powder and solutions of it in water. The sacks must be stored in a dry area and not allowed to become damp or mix with any other chemical. Stand the sack in use in a plastic dustbin.

The addition of kibbled alum (aluminium sulphate) is also used to assist filtration and is added immediately following each backwash of the filters, on the advice of Scientific Branch or DMEE.

Kibbled alum is normally supplied in 50 kg sacks. The solid is a skin irritant and dissolves in water to give an acidic solution which corrodes, and will cause skin burns and damage clothing on contact. Care should therefore be taken when handling this substance and *suitable protective clothing must be worn*.

1   What do you think would be 'suitable protective clothing' if you were handling kibbled alum?   *(1 mark)*

2   Which of the warning symbols would you expect to see:
   (a) on a cylinder of chlorine gas?
   (b) on a sack of soda ash?
   (c) on a sack of kibbled alum?   *(3 marks)*

3   Suppose you were writing a manual for swimming pool operators.
   (a) Using chlorine as an example, how would you explain to them the difference between a gas and a liquid?
   (b) How would you explain why the chlorine becomes a gas when the cylinder valve is opened?   *(3 marks)*
   Turn over (question continues)

A

B

C

D

E

F

G

4 Soda ash is added to swimming pool water to raise the pH.
  (a) What *type* of substance must soda ash be? *(1 mark)*
  (b) Name one product you would expect to be formed when soda ash is used in this way. *(2 marks)*

5 How could you check when enough soda ash had been added? *(1 mark)*

6 In some swimming pools, bromine is being used instead of chlorine. What do you know about bromine that makes it suitable for this purpose? *(2 marks)*

7 Copy and complete this table. (Relative atomic masses are given on the periodic table at the end of the book.)

Name	Formula	Mass of 1 mol/g	Mass in sack or cylinder/kg	Amount in sack or cylinder/mol
Soda ash	Na_2CO_3			
Chlorine	Cl_2			
Kibbled alum	$Al_2(SO_4)_3$			

(6 marks)

▶ 51 SWIMMING POOLS (B): HYGIENE

Read the following extracts, which come from an instruction manual for caretakers of swimming pools.

Chlorination

Why is correct chlorination of pool water so important?

(i) Inadequately treated pool water allows the spread of infections such as typhoid, dysentery, gastro-enteritis and poliomyelitis.

(ii) Ear and eye infection can also be transmitted when the pool water is incorrectly dosed. The organisms which cause this type of infection can survive low chlorine levels but are quickly killed off when the free chlorine is at 2 ppm in water at the correct pH value.

(iii) 'Swimming pool itch' occurs particularly in warm pools (80 °F and over), where the chlorine value is low and the pH is above pH 8.

Why is cleansing of floors so important?

(i) Unwashed floors can allow disease to spread. Some common infections are:

Athlete's Foot—a fungal infection particularly between toes;
Verrucae—wart-like growths due to a virus.

(ii) These can be spread from contact with floors of changing areas and bath surrounds. While exclusion of bathers with obvious foot infections is important, these problems can be contagious before actual physical signs are apparent. Prevention of spread must rely on frequent and thorough cleaning and disinfection of all areas where bare feet come into contact with surfaces.

(iii) Chronic skin ulcers are sometimes caused at pools especially where there are rough areas to tiling or surrounds. The bacteria which cause these ulcers grow in minor crevices and cracks, and enter the skin through scratches and abrasions caused by the rough surfaces. This problem is easily controlled by good pool maintenance, correct chlorination and adequate cleaning procedures.

The quality of the water depends on the capacity and efficiency of the purification plant and on the number of bathers using the pool. The water leaving the pool first passes through a coarse strainer which removes suspended matter (e.g., hairs, leaves, fibres etc.). It is then disinfected, filtered and returned to the pool.

1 Give the names of *two* infections that could be spread if the pool water was not adequately treated. *(2 marks)*

2 Give the names of *two* infections that could be spread by unwashed floors. *(2 marks)*

3 'Swimming pool itch' occurs if the pH rises above 8.
    (a) Is this pH acidic, neutral or alkaline? *(1 mark)*
    (b) What would you suggest doing if the pH rises above 8? *(1 mark)*

4 The chlorine level must be at least 2 ppm (parts per million) in water. That means 2 g Cl_2 in 1 000 000 cm³ water.
    (a) How many grams is this per litre (1 dm³) of water? *(1 mark)*
    (b) How many moles Cl_2 is this per litre of water? (Relative atomic masses are given on the periodic table at the end of the book.) *(1 mark)*
    (c) Would you consider this a concentrated or a dilute solution? *(1 mark)*
    (d) Suppose a swimming pool contains 400 m³ of water. Would one 50 kg cylinder of chlorine be sufficient to get the chlorine level to 2 ppm? Show your working. *(3 marks)*

Read this extract, which comes from an instruction manual for caretakers of swimming pools.

Some Pool Problems

SYMPTOM	CAUSE
Eyes red, water has an unpleasant odour, complaints of 'too much chlorine'	Insufficient chlorine! As the chlorine cleans the water it combines with ammonia-type chemicals, and is used up. New chemicals are made by this process. It is these chemicals (chloramines), not chlorine, that produce the symptoms
Eyes red, skin itching	Chloramines (as above)
Cloudy water	1 Early algae growth or 2 Poor filtration or 3 High pH or 4 Excessive use of alum
Eye irritation	Excessive chlorine
Water green and slippery feel to surfaces around pool. Spotty black patches on sides of pool	Insufficient chlorine

It is plain from the above that time honoured methods, such as using sore eyes to indicate that there is too much chlorine, are not satisfactory. Operatives should always rely on test readings to determine dosing needs.

1 What are the likely effects of too much chlorine in swimming pool water? *(1 mark)*

2 What are the likely effects of too little chlorine in swimming pool water? *(2 marks)*

3 The reaction between chlorine and ammonia could be written as:

$$Cl_2 + NH_3 \longrightarrow NH_2Cl + NH_4Cl$$

(a) Copy the above equation and balance it. *(1 mark)*

(b) What is the formula of chloramine? *(1 mark)*

(c) What is the name of the other product of this reaction? *(1 mark)*

(d) How do you suppose 'ammonia-type chemicals' get into swimming pool water? *(1 mark)*

(e) Both NH_2Cl and NH_4Cl dissolve in water, but only NH_4Cl produces a solution which conducts electricity. What does this tell you about the bonding in each? *(2 marks)*

▶ ## 53 SWIMMING POOLS (D): CHLORINE PROBLEMS

Chlorine Gas

Chlorine is a gas with a pungent smell (like bleach) and a greenish yellow colour. It is heavier than air and will tend to form a layer over the ground with strongest concentrations nearest the ground. (Never, therefore, leave a casualty lying on the ground in a contaminated area!) It will tend to fill hollows and low ground, cellars etc., and in the event of a leak such places should be avoided at all costs.

If a lot of chlorine has escaped an area may not have enough air to breathe and entry into such areas wearing a cannister type respirator can result in suffocation. Safe entry can only be made by use of breathing apparatus, and this means that the fire brigade must be called. Fortunately, the presence of chlorine is easily detected by its smell and the irritation it causes to eyes and nose. Thus in the event of serious leakage operatives will

usually have sufficient warning to escape from the area before serious exposure occurs.

Casualties should be exposed to fresh air and not permitted to exert themselves.

Breathing chlorine gas can produce delayed action effects and it is important that anyone so exposed should receive professional medical attention even if no ill effects are immediately apparent.

From an instruction manual for caretakers of swimming pools

1 Chlorine is said to smell like bleach. Why is this? *(1 mark)*

2 Why is it easy to detect a chlorine leak? *(1 mark)*

3 **(a)** Why must breathing apparatus be used if someone has to enter an area where there has been a chlorine leak?

(b) What do you think would be necessary as a part of that breathing apparatus? *(1 mark)*

4 Why would it be especially dangerous to enter cellars if there had been a chlorine leak? *(2 marks)*

5 Suppose you were planning a swimming pool for your school. What instructions would you give about the siting of the chlorine gas cylinders? *(2 marks)*

Sodium Hypochlorite Systems

INTRODUCTION

(i) Sodium hypochlorite solution is generally used as the disinfecting agent in the smaller pools, especially learner baths.

(ii) Swimming pools disinfected with sodium hypochlorite solution use two chemicals:

        (a) 10–14 % sodium hypochlorite solution;
        (b) 5 % hydrochloric acid solution.

(iii) When the water is disinfected with sodium hypochlorite solution, it tends to become alkaline (pH rises) and, unless corrected, this can lead to cloudiness in the pool water, and also result in less efficient disinfection. This is corrected by adding hydrochloric acid solution in order to maintain the pH value between 7.6–8.0.

(iv) Both the sodium hypochlorite solution and hydrochloric acid solution, suitably diluted, are injected into the pool water using appropriate dosing equipment

SODIUM HYPOCHLORITE SOLUTION (10–14%)—GENERAL

(i) Sodium hypochlorite solution 10–14 % is a pale greenish-yellow liquid, which smells like bleach. Only sodium hypochlorite solution specifically labelled 'For Swimming Pool Use' should be used.

(ii) The solution supplied contains a small quantity of caustic alkali, and needs to be handled with care. Suitable protective clothing must be worn when handling these containers, including eye goggles and gloves.

(iii) If sodium hypochlorite solution comes into contact with any acid, chlorine gas is produced, with possibly disastrous consequences. This can occur if hydrochloric acid, or certain lavatory cleaners or acid descalers are added to or accidentally mixed with the sodium hypochlorite solution. They must *not* be stored together.

(iv) Sodium hypochlorite solution is provided in clearly labelled *black coloured* plastic 5 litre containers. High temperatures quicken the deterioration of sodium hypochlorite, and it is recommended that storage is limited to the amount needed for efficient treatment and operation. Sodium hypochlorite should be stored in *cool conditions. It must never be allowed to stand in direct sunlight.* Under normal cool storage conditions, the solution deteriorates slowly and some gases are released. In view of this, the cap of the container is of a special self-venting type which will allow the gases to escape. Stock of sodium hypochlorite should not be kept longer than 2 months, if possible.

STORAGE BINS

Large galvanized storage bins for the bulk storage of sodium hypochlorite and hydrochloric acid containers have been provided. They should have been situated in a suitable position outside the school building protected from the sun (preferably north facing), raised from the ground and clearly marked according to the type of solution they contain.

The above extract comes from an instruction manual for caretakers of swimming pools. Read it carefully.

1 Which of the warning symbols below would you expect to find on a container of sodium hypochlorite? *(1 mark)*

A   B   C   D

E   F   G

2 **(a)** Why is it necessary to add hydrochloric acid to water disinfected with sodium hypochlorite? *(2 marks)*

(b) What would happen if too much hydrochloric acid were added? *(1 mark)*

(c) Sodium hypochlorite has the formula NaOCl, and hydrochloric acid is HCl. When they react, products include sodium chloride and water. Write a complete balanced equation for this reaction. *(2 marks)*

3 Why is it necessary for containers of sodium hypochlorite to have 'special self-venting' caps? *(2 marks)*

4 Explain why storage bins for sodium hypochlorite containers should preferably be north-facing. *(2 marks)*

▶ 55 SWIMMING POOLS (F): WATER CONDITION

Read this extract, which comes from an instruction manual for caretakers of swimming pools.

Water Condition and Testing Frequency

GENERAL

(i) The swimming pool water must *at all times* be crystal-clear, of good colour, attractive in appearance and be safe to swim in.

(ii) The water must be regularly treated with disinfectant and pH adjusting chemicals, to maintain the following levels:

  (a) free chlorine—1–3 mg/litre (ppm) (ideally 2–3 mg/litre);
  (b) pH—7.5–8.0.

(iii) The pool water must be tested at least 4 times a day at the following times:
  (a) As early as possible in the morning (i.e., before 8 am);
  (b) immediately prior to swimming (i.e., 9–9.30 am);
  (c) lunch time (just prior to swimming for the afternoon session);
  (d) late afternoon (after swimming has finished);
  (e) if swimming continues into the evening (e.g., for evening classes), then at least one further test should be made after swimming has finished.

(iv) It is important that a minimum of 1 mg/l (ppm) of free chlorine is maintained in the pool water *at all times*. To ensure that this level is present overnight, the free chlorine level in the pool water should be increased during the last two hours of swimming to a maximum of 4 mg/l.

(v) In order to maintain a minimum free chlorine level of 1 mg/l over the weekend, it may be necessary to treat the pool with chlorine disinfectant through the dosing equipment during Sunday.

1   What method would be used to obtain water which is 'crystal-clear'?   *(1 mark)*

2   **(a)** Why must the free chlorine not drop below 1 mg/litre?
                                              (1 mark)

  (b) Why must the free chlorine not normally rise above 3 mg/litre?   *(1 mark)*

  (c) Why do you think it is necessary to boost the level of chlorine to 4 mg/litre during the last 2 hours of swimming?   *(1 mark)*

3   The pool has to be tested at least four times a day to ensure that the pH is correct.

(a) Describe carefully how *you* would expect to do this.
(2 marks)

(b) In fact, normal procedures cannot be used, because chlorine would bleach the indicator. Why would this matter? *(1 mark)*

4 Chlorine produces a red colour with DPD tablets: the more chlorine, the stronger the colour. Use this idea to devise a possible way of measuring the amount of chlorine in a swimming pool. Say what equipment you would use, how you would use it, what you would measure, and how you would interpret the results. *(3 marks)*

▶ 56   RUBBISH BINS

The picture shows a steel rubbish bin. The steel has been coated with a thin layer of zinc: the zinc shows up as feathery patterns.

1 Explain what steel is. *(1 mark)*

2 **(a)** Suggest two reasons why steel is a good choice for making rubbish bins. *(2 marks)*

(b) Suggest one reason why steel is *not* a good choice for making rubbish bins. *(1 mark)*

3 **(a)** Explain why the steel is coated with zinc. *(2 marks)*

(b) What word is used to describe steel that has been coated with zinc in this way? *(1 mark)*

4 State two methods by which a thin coating of zinc such as this might be applied to the steel. *(2 marks)*

5 The feathery patterns of zinc on the surface are, in fact, zinc crystals. Explain what is meant by the word crystal. *(2 marks)*

6 Suppose you were coating steel with zinc in a school laboratory, and you wanted to know how thick a coating you had applied. Devise a method of measuring the thickness: say what you would do, what you would measure, and make clear any assumptions you would make. *(3 marks)*

► 57 ETHANOL AS FUEL

The article on the next page appeared in the *Guardian*, on 20 February 1987, as part of a feature about Malawi, a country in Central Africa.

1 Give the names of three chemicals which this advertisement states can be made from ethanol. *(3 marks)*

2 What is meant by the word 'fuel'? *(1 mark)*

3 If ethanol burns, what products would you expect to be formed? *(2 marks)*

4 Ethanol and petrol mix readily with each other. What does this tell you about the type of bonding present in both substances? *(1 mark)*

5 Why is it an advantage for Malawi to be able to mix its petrol with ethanol? *(1 mark)*

6 From what starting material does Malawi make its ethanol? *(1 mark)*

7 How is ethanol made from this starting material? *(1 mark)*

8 The photograph below shows a distillation plant. What does this do, and why is it necessary. *(3 marks)*

Distillation plant adjacent the cane fields

Ethanol: Malawi's Versatile Fuel

The versatility of ethanol as a fuel is not well known. It has many applications in the fuel industry and these are being investigated in Malawi. Ethanol has many derivatives, which have diverse uses in the chemical and pharmaceutical industries. Ethylene, a basic component in plastics, acetic acid (vinegar) and ethylacetate (an industrial solvent) are but a few examples of its important place and versatility in the chemical industry. It is for this reason that the Ethanol Company in Malawi is embarking on a programme to show its versatility and thus its importance in the economy.

Ethanol Company Limited was established in Malawi in 1980 and at the outset tribute must be paid to His Excellency the Life President, Ngwazi Dr H. Kamuzu Banda, whose wisdom and vision conceived the project.

Malawi is among some 50 countries in the world producing and using fuel ethanol, and one of the first in the world to have a national blend of 20 % ethanol in its petrol.

Due to the high cost of imported petroleum products in most developing countries, the value and versatility of ethanol is receiving more attention. Malawi is in the forefront, as it is investigating seven distinct areas of additional utilization of this locally produced product.

Not only does the ethanol displace imported fuel but, due to one of its characteristics (that of an octane improver), a lower-octane-level petrol can be imported, and ethanol blended to make the premium (high octane) motor fuel required in Malawi.

Ethanol's use as a blend component in petrol is well known. Motor car engines suitable for pure ethanol fuel are being produced in Brazil at the rate of over half a million a year. Early cars at the turn of the century ran on ethanol.

What is probably not so well known is that ethanol can be used as a blend component in diesel. This application is more difficult than petrol ethanol blends, but there has been success in many parts of the world, particularly in the agriculture sector. This augurs well for Malawi's agricultural economy. The Ethanol Company tractor has been running on a 15 % ethanol in diesel blend for 4 years with no ill effects.

A synthetic diesel can be produced from ethanol with an 'ignition improving' additive. Trials have been successful in other parts of the world. Ethanol Company is carrying out similar trials under local conditions.

Ethanol can be used for heating, lighting and refrigeration in a similar way to paraffin. This aspect is currently receiving considerable attention in Malawi as this could benefit the rural areas.

As ethanol is produced from agricultural raw material (sugar or starch or cellulose), it is an ideal product for an agricultural-based economy such as Malawi's, and its variety of uses will soon be benefitting the economy. Not only does ethanol production save foreign exchange by displacing imports, but Malawi is exporting certain grades of ethanol to SADCC and PTA countries. Enquiries are being received from around the world on the progress of the Malawi Ethanol utilization programme.

► 58   SODIUM COOLANT

It often surprises chemistry students to learn that sodium is used as a heat transfer fluid (a coolant) in some nuclear power stations.

1   Suppose the leaking sodium had caught fire.
   (a) Why would you not use water to put it out?   *(1 mark)*
   (b) What fire-fighting method would you suggest? Why?
   (2 marks)

2   The following are all true statements about sodium:

   A   as it is a metal, it conducts heat well
   B   as it is a metal, it conducts electricity well
   C   although it is a metal, it melts at low temperatures
   D   it is a very reactive metal
   E   virtually all of its compounds dissolve easily in water

Which of these five properties, A to E, are important for sodium's use as a coolant in nuclear power stations? Explain why each of the properties you select is important.   *(4 marks)*

3   This nuclear reactor contains about 690 tonnes of sodium.
   (a) From what readily available and cheap raw material would the sodium have been made?   *(1 mark)*
   (b) What other useful material would be produced as a by-product when making the sodium?   *(1 mark)*
   (c) Calculate how much of the raw material you would need to start with in order to obtain 690 tonnes of sodium. (Relative atomic masses are given on the periodic table at the end of the book.)   *(2 marks)*

▶ 59 PLASTIC RUBBISH

Read this extract from a longer newspaper article concerning our use of scarce resources. The article appeared in *The Observer* on 19 April, 1987.

1 'The oil…took hundreds of millions of years to form and cannot be replaced.'
  (a) How was the oil formed?   *(2 marks)*
  (b) Why can't oil be replaced?   *(1 mark)*

2 The author suggests that the plastic shopping bag is made from oil. So it is—as a result of a complicated series of processes, represented by this flow diagram:

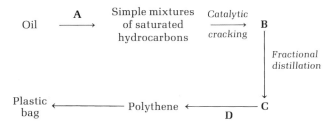

  (a) What processes are represented by **A** and **D**?
                                                    (2 marks)
  (b) What substances are represented by **B** and **C**?
                                                    (2 marks)

3 **(a)** Why would a polythene bag 'swell the world's growing garbage mountain', whereas a paper bag would not?
                                                    (1 mark)
   (b) Polythene is a hydrocarbon. Why can't it be disposed of by burning?
                                                    (2 marks)

4 **(a)** If **O** represents styrene, how would you represent polystyrene?
                                                    (1 mark)
   (b) Gas is used to 'puff up' polystyrene when making hamburger boxes. What is the advantage of having foamed polystyrene?
                                                    (1 mark)

5 The author is arguing that using plastics for packaging is a waste of our resources. Do you agree? Write a letter to the newspaper:
   either supporting the view, and suggesting what should be done;
   or opposing the view, arguing how useful plastics are.
                                                    (5 marks)

CONSIDER, if you will, the humble plastic shopping bag. The oil from which it is made took hundreds of millions of years to form and cannot be replaced. The bag will be in use for perhaps an hour or two. Then it will be thrown away.

If it ends up on a rubbish dump, it will swell the world's growing garbage mountain (half of US cities will run out of their existing tipping space by 1990). Generations hence it will still be intact. If, in an attempt to beat the garbage crisis, it is burned in a municipal incineration plant, it will give off dioxins—among the most feared pollutants in the world.

Or take those natty polystyrene foam boxes used for hamburgers and other fast food. Their useful life is measured in minutes. Yet they pose the same questions about the use of resources and the production of pollution—with one added complication. For when they are broken they release the gases used to puff them up—and these threaten to change the world's climate and seriously deplete the world's life-saving ozone layer which screens out harmful ultraviolet rays of the sun.

And how about the ubiquitous aerosol can? The gas used to squirt out instant freshness and spray-on sex appeal does its job in seconds. Yet it, too, slowly drifts up to the stratosphere to help heat the climate and let in more ultraviolet radiation, to cause millions of extra cases of skin-cancer over the years—often on the very bodies it was used to beautify.

▶ 60–61 ACID RAIN

The top photograph shows part of the wall of a church built of sandstone. The church was built over a hundred years ago, and since then it has suffered much damage as a result of acid rain.

▶ 60 ACID RAIN (A)

1 **(a)** Explain what is meant by acid rain, and how it is formed. *(3 marks)*
  (b) Apart from damaging building stones, what other problems can acid rain cause? *(2 marks)*

2 Sandstone consists of grains of silicon dioxide joined together by calcium carbonate. Acid has no effect on silicon dioxide.
  (a) What effect would acid have on calcium carbonate? *(2 marks)*
  (b) What effect would acid rain have on sandstone? *(2 marks)*

3 This kerbstone is just next to the church, and has been there about as long. It is made of granite, and is undamaged. What does this tell you about the chemical composition of granite? *(1 mark)*

4 How would you investigate, in a school laboratory, which building stones (concrete, brick, sandstone, limestone, etc.) were most at risk of damage by acid rain? Say what you would do, what equipment you would use, and what you would look for. (A convenient way of making sulphur dioxide in the laboratory is by adding an acid to sodium sulphite.) *(5 marks)*

▶ 61 ACID RAIN (B)

One of the constituents of acid rain is sulphur dioxide. The following table shows the amount of sulphur dioxide, during the summer and winter months, as measured by Westminster City Council at a site close to the church.

1 Why do local authorities measure pollutants such as sulphur dioxide? *(2 marks)*

Year	Summer SO_2 /μg m^{-3}	Winter SO_2 /μg m^{-3}
1965	130	361
1966	148	239
1967	151	224
1968	137	254
1969	137	271
1970	133	212
1971	125	205
1972	150	188
1973	115	207
1974	135	173
1975	110	148
1976	—	175
1977	80	124
1978	66	120
1979	80	144
1980	77	108
1981	69	71

The data show the average concentration of SO_2 in micrograms per cubic metre, during the summer (April to September) and winter months. No figure for summer 1976 is available.

2 Plot, on the same set of axes, two graphs, showing the year (along the bottom), and the seasonal concentrations of sulphur dioxide. (You may find a convenient scale is 1 cm = 1 year, and 1 cm = 20 μg m^{-3}.) *(5 marks)*

3 No figure is available for the summer of 1976. Use your graph to make an estimate. *(1 mark)*

4 Explain why the summer and winter figures are different. *(2 marks)*

5 Explain why the concentration of sulphur dioxide (both summer and winter) has changed over the years. *(2 marks)*

6 What, if anything, do you think can and should be done about acid rain? Bring as many scientific facts as possible into your arguments. *(4 marks)*

► 62 UNLEADED PETROL

The information leaflet on the next page was produced by Esso in 1987.

1   **(a)** Petrol is usually described as a hydrocarbon. What does this mean? *(1 mark)*

      (b) How is petrol obtained from crude oil? *(1 mark)*

2   **(a)** Why did most of the petrol sold in the UK in 1987 contain lead? *(1 mark)*

      (b) What do you think happens to the lead in petrol when the petrol is burnt in a car engine? *(1 mark)*

      (c) Why was the amount of lead in petrol reduced from January 1986, with further reductions planned? *(1 mark)*

3   Lead is added to petrol in the form of lead tetraethyl, $Pb(C_2H_5)_4$.

      (a) What is the mass of 1 mole of lead tetraethyl? (Relative atomic masses are given on the periodic table at the end of the book.) *(1 mark)*

      (b) If a litre of petrol contains 0.15 g lead, what mass of lead tetraethyl does it contain? *(2 marks)*

UNLEADED PETROL
Questions and Answers

1

Q What is "Unleaded" Petrol?
A It is petrol to which no lead has been deliberately added.

2

Q Why is lead added to petrol?
A Small quantities of lead compounds can be added to petrol to increase its octane number. This allows the use of higher compression ratio engines with more ingnition spark advance, which means improved engine efficiency and fuel economy. To replace lead we have to introduce more high octane compounds to compensate.

3

Q How much lead is added currently to normal leaded petrol?
A The content can vary but it will not exceed 0.15g per litre.

4

Q What is 'low lead' petrol compared to 'Unleaded'?
A 'Low Lead' refers to the normal leaded petrol which is currently available. This is because the lead content was reduced in all petrol to 0.15g per litre on 1st January 1986 from its previous level of 0.40g per litre, in line with British Standard 4040. 'Unleaded' petrol is allowed to contain up to 0.013g per litre which is why it cannot be called 'lead free,' although on the Continent this term may be used where 'Unleaded' cannot be translated.

5

Q Can I use 'Unleaded' petrol in my car?
A The majority of cars in the United Kingdom have been designed to run on leaded petrol. However, nearly 40% of post 1985 petrol cars are now capable of running on 'Unleaded' fuel, although most will need some minor adjustments to allow this. Eventually all new petrol cars will incorporate the necessary modifications for them to run on 'Unleaded.' Before attempting to use unleaded petrol you should check first with your car dealer or motor manufacturer.

6

Q What is a 'catalytic convertor'?
A A catalytic convertor is a device that can be fitted to the exhaust system. When the exhaust fumes pass through the convertor, emissions such as nitrogen oxide and carbon monoxide are burnt up or oxidised. Unfortunately, lead damages the catalysts, so they are only effective on cars already using 'Unleaded' petrol.

LEAPING FORWARD WITH UNLEADED.

These questions relate to extracts from a guidebook to the famous mineral springs in Buxton, Derbyshire.

► 63 BUXTON'S THERMAL SPRINGS (A)

St Ann's Well, Buxton

A thousand feet above sea level are medicinal springs known to the Romans, who called the place 'Aquae'. But their existence, like those at Bath, was almost forgotten for centuries.

The springs are of two kinds. The thermal water emerges from the limestone rock by nine springs, outlets from the same subterranean reservoir where the water lies for at least twenty years before rising to the surface. From one of these springs alone approximately 2 000 000 litres flow daily at a constant temperature of 82°F (28°C). The water when seen in depth is beautifully clear and blue, with bubbles of gas constantly rising to discharge on the surface. This gas consists chiefly of nitrogen and carbon dioxide, but also contains argon and helium. It is the vehicle of the radium-emanation to which the name radon has been given.

1 Why are these referred to as 'thermal' springs? *(1 mark)*

2 **(a)** Draw up a table listing the gases which bubble up from the springs. For each gas in the mixture, show in your table whether it is an element or a compound. Put a number '1' in the table for the gas you consider the most reactive, '2' for the next most reactive, and so on. *(4 marks)*

   (b) Explain how you chose your numbers '1', '2', etc., for the reactivity of these gases. *(2 marks)*

   (c) If you tested the mixture of gases with an indicator, what pH would you expect? Why? *(2 marks)*

3 Suppose you collected a sample of the gas bubbling up from the spring. How could you measure how much of the gas was carbon dioxide? Describe what you would do, what apparatus you would use, and how you would work out your results. *(3 marks)*

4 Helium has a variety of uses.

    (a) State one use for helium. *(1 mark)*

    (b) Suppose a manufacturer wanted to obtain helium from the mixture bubbling up at the springs. State how s/he might be able to separate it from the other gases present. *(2 marks)*

▶ 64 BUXTON'S THERMAL SPRINGS (B)

This table shows the amounts (in mg per 1000 litres) of different ions in Buxton's spring water.

Positive ions	mg/1000 l
Calcium	58.0
Barium	0.5
Magnesium	18.9
Iron	0.09
Aluminium	0.38
Manganese	0.11
Sodium	20.5
Potassium	3.8
Armonium	trace

Negative ions	
Bicarbonate	228.1
Sulphate	10.4
Chloride	38.7
Silicate	14.5
Iodide	4.4

1   **(a)** What is the most abundant positive ion present? *(1 mark)*

    (b) Which of the ions present would carry a charge of $3+$? *(1 mark)*

    (c) Which is the most abundant of the ions carrying a charge of $1+$? *(1 mark)*

    (d) There is a misprint in the name of one of the positive ions: what should it read? *(1 mark)*

2   Bicarbonate ions are obviously abundant. They get into the water when calcium carbonate is dissolved according to the following equation:

$$CaCO_3 + H_2O + CO_2 \rightleftharpoons Ca^{2+} + 2HCO_3^-$$

    (a) Copy down this equation, and put in the appropriate symbols of state [(s), (l), (g), (aq)]. *(2 marks)*

    (b) In what form is the calcium carbonate found in the Buxton area? *(1 mark)*

    (c) Explain the meaning of the symbol $\rightleftharpoons$. *(1 mark)*

3   **(a)** Explain what difference you would expect between the behaviour of calcium atoms and calcium ions. *(2 marks)*

    (b) An earlier table of the constituents of the spring water referred to magnesium bicarbonate, calcium sulphate, magnesium sulphate, etc. Explain why such a list is not really as accurate as a list of the ions. *(2 marks)*

    (c) Suppose you were writing a guidebook to Buxton's springs for the general public. Write a few sentences to explain what an 'ion' is. *(3 marks)*

▶ 65 WASHING POWDERS

Most washing powders used these days are fairly complicated mixtures, but they will all contain a *detergent* and biological washing powders will also contain *enzymes*.

1   **(a)** Why is a washing powder which contains enzymes called a 'biological' washing powder?   *(1 mark)*
    (b) Explain the job that the enzyme does.   *(2 marks)*
    (c) Biological washing powders should not be used in very hot water. Why not?   *(1 mark)*

2   Many different detergents may be found in modern washing powders, but most consist of a sodium salt attached to a long hydrocarbon chain.
    (a) Copy the diagram, which represents the structure of a detergent. Mark on it the part that shows the hydrocarbon chain, and the part that shows the sodium salt.   *(1 mark)*
    (b) Given a sample of Bold 3, what simple test would you carry out to see if it does, in fact, contain a sodium compound?   *(2 marks)*

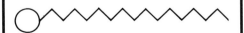

The structure of a detergent

E3 SIZE AUTOMATIC WASHING POWDER WITH BIOLOGICAL ACTION AND BLEACHING AND BRIGHTENING AGENTS

(c) Which part of the detergent would you expect to dissolve most easily in water: the hydrocarbon chain, or the sodium salt? Explain how you arrive at your answer. *(2 marks)*

(d) Use the idea that one part of the detergent dissolves easily in water and the other part does not to explain, with the help of diagrams, how a detergent can get clothes clean. *(3 marks)*

3 If you were given a packet of Bold 3 and a packet of ordinary biological powder, how would you investigate whether the claim 'It cleans first time, more of the time' was actually true? Say what you would do, what equipment you would use, how you would make your tests fair, and how you would interpret your results. *(4 marks)*

▶ 66 VACUUM FLASK

Look at the information from the packaging around a popular make of vacuum flask.

1 **(a)** What advantage do vacuum flasks have over other containers? *(1 mark)*

(b) Where is the vacuum in a vacuum flask? *(1 mark)*

2 Bicarbonate of soda is a common kitchen chemical. Describe experiments that you would do to check the claim that it can be used to remove deposits from a vacuum flask. Say what you would do, how you would do it, how you would interpret your results, and what you would do to make sure the test was fair. *(3 marks)*

3 The deposit on the inside of a vacuum flask might be calcium carbonate.

(a) How might calcium carbonate get there? *(1 mark)*

(b) What simple test would you carry out to check that the deposit was a carbonate of some sort? *(2 marks)*

4 **(a)** Sodium is in Group 1 of the periodic table. What would you expect the formula of a sodium ion to be? *(1 mark)*

(b) The hydrogencarbonate ion has the formula $(HCO_3)^-$. What would you expect the formula of sodium hydrogencarbonate to be? *(1 mark)*

(c) The label refers to 'bicarbonate of soda $(Na(HCO_3)_2)$'. What is odd about this? *(1 mark)*

(d) Write a letter to the makers of these vacuum flasks, explaining why you think they have made a mistake on their label. *(3 marks)*

THERMOS
REGISTERED TRADE MARK

**THERMOS LIMITED
BRENTWOOD, ESSEX,
ENGLAND.**

TO CLEAN THE INSIDE OF YOUR VACUUM FLASK
A solution of bicarbonate of soda $(Na(HCO_3)_2)$ in hot water will remove surface deposit inside the filler if left overnight.

Compare these three toothpaste boxes.

FLUORIDE
TOOTHPASTE

HELPS PROTECT TEETH FROM DECAY
FRESHMINT FLAVOUR

TESCO 28p ■

50 ml

Research has proved that regular brushing with a Fluoride Toothpaste helps prevent tooth decay and helps protect teeth and gums from plaque. Plaque is the build-up of bacterial film which forms around the margin where tooth and gum meet, and is the primary cause of dental disease and disorder. Tesco Fluoride Toothpaste has been formulated with a bactericide and special ingredients to help fight plaque and protect your teeth, keeping them clean and healthy.

■ ACTIVE INGREDIENTS. 0.85% Sodium Monofluorophosphate
0.1% Cetyl Pyridinium Chloride

PRODUCED IN THE U.K. FOR TESCO STORES LTD CHESHUNT HERTS 50 ml ℮

5 000119 124920

ORIGINAL Minty Fresh

Crest ✚

Crest

Clinically tested toothpaste

Active ingredient 0.24% sodium fluoride by weight.
Made in England by PROCTER & GAMBLE LIMITED, Newcastle upon Tyne.
IRELAND write to Crest, Box 596, Dublin 14. ΟΔΟΝΤΟΚΡΕΜΑ ΑΓΓΛΙΚΗΣ
ΠΑΡΑΓΩΓΗΣ - ΠΡΟΚΤΕΡ & ΓΚΑΜΠΛ ΕΛΛΑΣ Α.Ε. - ΣΥΓΓΡΟΥ 165 - ΑΘΗΝΑ - ΕΟΦ

ΚΕΝΤΡΟ ΔΗΛΗΤΗΡΙΑΣΕΩΝ 7793-777

For best results
1. Have old tartar removed by your Dentist.
2. Brush regularly with Tartar Control Crest+ to help stop new tartar from forming above the gumline and help protect your teeth against decay.
3. Continue to see your Dentist regularly.

5017 4423

FLUORIDE + <u>CALCIUM G.P.</u>

FRESHMINT
macleans
UNBEATABLE DECAY PREVENTION

CLINICALLY PROVEN TO BE BETTER
In an independent clinical trial **Macleans** with Fluoride plus Calcium G.P. has been CLINICALLY PROVEN TO BE BETTER than with fluoride alone.

UNIQUE FORMULATION
Macleans has a unique formulation with Fluoride plus Calcium G.P. which offers you: UNBEATABLE DECAY PREVENTION AND PROTECTION AGAINST PLAQUE – the cause of gum disease.

TWO FLAVOURS
Macleans is available in two great flavours – original FRESHMINT and refreshing, cool MILDMINT.
macleans
NO BETTER PROTECTION FOR YOUR FAMILY'S TEETH.

5 000199 051727

Contains sodium monofluorophosphate 0.8% w/w and calcium glycerophosphate 0.13% w/w Patent No GB 1384375 **PL|0079|0196** Beecham Proprietaries, Brentford, England

1 **(a)** One of the toothpastes contains a calcium compound. Which toothpaste, and what is the chemical name of the compound? *(2 marks)*

(b) Suggest why it might be helpful to have calcium compounds in toothpaste. *(1 mark)*

2 Two of the toothpastes contain sodium monofluoro-phosphate, Na_2PO_3F. Which toothpaste contains the greater percentage? *(1 mark)*

3 The third toothpaste contains a different fluorine compound, sodium fluoride, NaF. Suppose your grandad read, quite correctly, that fluorine is a dangerously poisonous and reactive element, similar to, but worse than, chlorine. How would you explain to him that these toothpastes, containing fluorine compounds, were quite safe to use? *(4 marks)*

4 **(a)** In 1000 g of Macleans, there would be 8 g Na_2PO_3F. How many grams of NaF would there be in 1000 g of Crest? *(1 mark)*

(b) In 1000 g of toothpaste, would you get more fluorine with Crest or Macleans? Show how you arrive at your answer. (Relative atomic masses are given at the end of the book.) *(3 marks)*

Some people need to remove the 'scale' from the insides of their kettles and coffee machines.

▶ 68   SCALE REMOVER (A)

1   Why do you think the label says, 'Keep out of reach of children'?   *(1 mark)*

2   **(a)** What is the chemical composition of scale?   *(1 mark)*
    (b) Explain carefully how scale gets deposited on the insides of kettles and similar containers.   *(2 marks)*
    (c) Which parts of the country would be most likely to suffer from scale formation?   *(1 mark)*

3   Explain how removing scale might 'save electricity' and 'increase the life of your machine'.   *(2 marks)*

4   Explain carefully why an acid can be used to remove scale.   *(1 mark)*

5   **(a)** The label suggests that care must be taken not to pour the sulphamic acid onto plated surfaces, i.e., it must not be poured onto certain metals. Explain what would happen if the acid came into contact with such metals.   *(2 marks)*
    (b) Most kettles are made of metal. Why does it not matter if the acid comes into contact with this metal?   *(1 mark)*

▶ 69   SCALE REMOVER (B)

1   What is the mass of 1 mole of sulphamic acid, NH_2SO_3H? (Relative atomic masses are given at the end of the book.)   *(1 mark)*

2   How many moles of sulphamic acid are contained in the packet of Quick Descaler?   *(1 mark)*

3   The packet is to be dissolved in 1 pint of water. Take 1 pint as $570\,cm^3$, and thus work out the concentration of the sulphamic acid solution in $mol\,dm^{-3}$ (i.e. calculate its molarity).   *(2 marks)*

4   **(a)** Write a word equation for the reaction between scale and sulphamic acid, giving the correct chemical name for scale.   *(2 marks)*
    (b) Write a balanced chemical equation for the reaction between scale and sulphamic acid. (Only one of the hydrogen atoms in sulphamic acid is replaceable by a metal.) Include state symbols in your equation.   *(3 marks)*

Compare these two cold relief treatments.

Complete Cold | Treatment-*Fast*

Lemsip is the complete way to relieve your cold and flu symptoms fast and make you feel more comfortable. Its approved cold relief actions – antipyretic to lower temperature; analgesic, to relieve headache and soothe body aches and pains; decongestant, to clear a stuffy nose and ease catarrh; and expectorant to calm a cough, provide a complete cold treatment. Lemsip contains whole real lemon (not just an extract) and added Vitamin C so it's pleasant to take for colds and flu, day or night. Taken piping hot especially at bedtime, Lemsip's warmth soon makes you feel more comfortable. Take it for summer colds too.

DIRECTIONS: Pour contents of one sachet into a beaker and fill with hot water. Stir until dissolved and sweeten to taste. The dose may be repeated after 4 hours, but do not take more than 4 doses in 24 hours. Do not exceed the stated dose. If symptoms persist, consult your doctor. If you are receiving medicines from your doctor consult him before taking Lemsip. Do not give to children under 12 except on medical advice. Junior Lemsip is specially formulated for children aged 3-12.

INGREDIENTS: Each Lemsip sachet contains: Paracetamol Ph. Eur. 650 mg, Phenylephrine Hydrochloride BP 5 mg, Sodium Citrate Ph. Eur. 500 mg, Ascorbic Acid Ph. Eur. (Vitamin C) 10 mg in a base containing whole real lemon.

CONTAINS PARACETAMOL   Store in a cool place   P

 KEEP ALL MEDICINES OUT OF THE REACH OF CHILDREN.

 Made in Britain
Reckitt & Colman Pharmaceutical Division, Hull.
Export Distributors: Reckitt & Colman (Overseas) Ltd., Hull.
PL 44/5005 ∝   669422

BLACKCURRANT ✚ FLAVOURED JUNIOR LEMSIP REGD

A child's measured dose for fast cold relief

Blackcurrant Flavoured Junior Lemsip, in a child's measured dose provides the complete way to relieve a child's cold symptoms and make him feel more comfortable. Its approved cold relief actions — antipyretic to lower temperature; analgesic, to relieve headache and soothe body aches and pains; decongestant, to clear a stuffy nose and ease catarrh; and expectorant to calm a cough, provide a complete cold treatment. Blackcurrant Flavoured Junior Lemsip contains real blackcurrant and lemon (not just extracts) and added Vitamin 'C' so it is pleasant to take and a flavour children like. Let him sip it hot and he will soon feel more comfortable. Give it for summer colds too.

DIRECTIONS: Children 3 — under 6 years: 1 sachet. Children 6 — under 12 years: 2 sachets. Pour contents of sachet into a small beaker and half fill with hot water (not boiling). For 2 sachets fill the beaker. Stir until dissolved and sweeten to taste. The dose may be repeated after 4 hours, but do not give more than 4 doses in 24 hours. Do not exceed the stated dose. Do not give for more than 3 days without consulting a doctor. If symptoms persist consult your doctor. Do not give to children under 3 except on medical advice. If your child has been prescribed a medicine by a doctor consult him before administering Blackcurrant Flavoured Junior Lemsip.

INGREDIENTS: Each Blackcurrant Flavoured Junior Lemsip sachet contains: Paracetamol Ph Eur 217mg, Phenylephrine Hydrochloride BP 1.7mg, Sodium Citrate Ph Eur 167mg, Ascorbic Acid Ph Eur (Vitamin 'C') 3.3mg. In a base containing whole real blackcurrant and lemon.

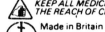 *KEEP ALL MEDICINES OUT OF THE REACH OF CHILDREN*

Made in Britain   CONTAINS PARACETAMOL   STORE IN A COOL PLACE
Reckitt & Colman, Pharmaceutical Division, Hull PL 44/0027
Export Distributors: Reckitt & Colman (Overseas) Ltd, Hull

1 Draw up a table to compare the ingredients in these two treatments. Arrange your table like this:

Ingredient	Lemsip	Junior Lemsip

(3 marks)

2 What is another name for vitamin C? *(1 mark)*

3 **(a)** Why do both packets state, 'Keep all medicines out of the reach of children'? *(1 mark)*

(b) How is it that one of these treatments is described as 'A child's measured dose...', when elsewhere on the label, it says 'Keep all medicines out of the reach of children'? *(1 mark)*

4 Suppose that a sachet of each of these was dissolved in separate portions of distilled water, and sodium hydroxide solution was then added to each, a little at a time. Which would require more sodium hydroxide to produce a neutral solution? Explain how you arrive at your answer. *(2 marks)*

5 How would you attempt to show that there is about three times as much ascorbic acid in a sachet of Lemsip as in a sachet of Junior Lemsip? *(2 marks)*

6 What steps do you think a pharmaceutical company must take before it can market a new drug or medicine? *(3 marks)*

▶ 71–72 ACID RAIN IN ATHENS

Read this article about the effects of acid rain on 2000-year-old statues and buildings in Athens.

Every time it rains in Athens, it rains dilute sulphuric acid, and a little bit more of the Acropolis disappears. The ancient marble has suffered more during the last thirty years than it had during the two thousand that preceded them. Ecologists will be familiar with the simple chemical formula: industrial chimneys, heating and transport fuel, all give off sulphurous fumes which hit the atmosphere as sulphur dioxide (SO_2).

Mixed with another atom of oxygen and then dissolved by rain (HO), it comes down as dilute sulphuric acid (HSO_4) and does what the Franks, Venetians and Turks, who all left their mark on the temple of Athens, could never manage. It makes the marble crumble.

This type of pollution is a phenomenon to some extent common to all industrialized countries, but since Athens has some of the worst air pollution in western Europe, it suffers more than most. According to one recent survey, 150 000 tons of sulphur dioxide are pumped into the Athenian air every year.

The Caryatids* are in a very bad way. If they continue to be exposed to the polluted elements, their features will soon be obliterated, and they are now too far gone to be preserved *in situ*.

An international panel of experts has decided that they can only be saved by removing them to the Acropolis Museum and replacing them with replicas made out of cement and marble dust. The cast for the replicas has already been prepared by the British Museum from the Caryatid Lord Elgin removed to England over 100 years ago, which is in much better condition. But taking the figures down without damaging them is a complicated task, and Mr George Dontas, the Director of the Acropolis, thinks it unlikely that it will be completed before the end of the year. In the meantime, the Caryatids will be sealed where they are in glass and steel boxes filled with nitrogen gas, to keep them at constant temperature.

(*The Caryatids are a set of marble statues.)

Observer, 15 January 1978

▶ 71 ACID RAIN IN ATHENS (A)

1 The pH of clean rain water is about 5.5. What do you think the pH of rain water in Athens might be? *(1 mark)*

2 **(a)** How do you know, from this newspaper article, that there has been a dramatic increase in pollution in Athens since the 1940s? *(1 mark)*

(b) Suggest why pollution has increased dramatically since the 1940s. *(1 mark)*

(c) This article appeared in 1978. Would you expect the situation now to be better, worse or much the same? Explain your reasons. *(2 marks)*

3 **(a)** What is the *main type* of chemical compound present in heating and transport fuel? *(1 mark)*

(b) Why do heating and transport fuels give off 'sulphurous fumes' when they burn? *(1 mark)*

4 Give the name of one other pollutant, which is *not* a sulphur compound, which you would expect to find in the air in Athens and explain how it gets there. *(2 marks)*

5 Apart from making buildings and statues crumble, state one other problem that is likely to be caused by air pollution in Athens. *(1 mark)*

6 **(a)** What gas, other than nitrogen, could have been used to protect the statues in their glass and steel boxes? *(1 mark)*

(b) Why would this gas have been equally suitable? *(1 mark)*

▶ 72 ACID RAIN IN ATHENS (B)

1 The three chemical formulae have been wrongly printed in this newspaper article. How should they be written? *(3 marks)*

2 Sulphur trioxide, SO_3, is formed when sulphur dioxide reacts with oxygen.

(a) Write a balanced equation for this reaction. *(2 marks)*

(b) From a chemist's point of view, explain what is wrong with the statement in the article: 'Mixed with another atom of oxygen ...' (line 13). *(2 marks)*

(c) '... and then dissolved by rain, it comes down as dilute sulphuric acid'. Write an equation for this, including symbols of state. *(2 marks)*

3 **(a)** Chemically speaking, what is marble? *(1 mark)*

(b) Why does sulphuric acid make the marble crumble? *(1 mark)*

(c) Write an equation for this reaction. *(1 mark)*

4 How much sulphur must be burnt every year in order to produce 150 000 tons of sulphur dioxide? (Relative atomic masses are listed at the end of this book.) *(2 marks)*

From the sweat of his brow

In the sweat of thy face shalt thou eat bread, was the prophecy accompanying the expulsion from the Garden of Eden. Jeff Bracey, a Merseyside pharmacist, has been making bread out of the sweat of other people's faces—and other parts.

He was running a successful pharmacy in an affluent suburb, when he was approached by a nursing sister who suffered from hyper-hydrosis. In English, that meant she sweated too much and suffered skin rashes, discomfort and embarrassment as a result, not least when she worked in the hot, stressful environment of an operating theatre.

As a favour, and a challenge, he looked up the subject in Liverpool University library and discovered that the answer, aluminium chloride, had been known for half a century. But so had its drawbacks, not least that it gave rise to molecules of corrosive hydrochloric acid in contact with water. And it absorbed water from the atmosphere, so even applying it in an alcohol base didn't totally eliminate the side effects of the acid on sensitive skin.

He was obviously a friendlier than average local chemist, since around the same time another customer came seeking advice on an apparently totally unrelated problem.

He made his own flies for fishing, and wanted a water repellent which would keep his artificial dry flies afloat and unbedraggled in the water. Jeff experimented with silicone preparations until he found the one—and realised that this was also the answer to the problems with his proto-anti-perspirant.

The mixture worked, and what's more, worked with remarkable efficacy. It lasted for a week per application without any embarrassingly corrosive side effects.

▶ 73 ANTI-PERSPIRANT

Read the extract from an article on anti-perspirants. The extract appeared in the business section of the newspaper.

1 Why is the fact that aluminium chloride produces hydrochloric acid in contact with moisture a drawback? *(1 mark)*

2 Why wouldn't it help if the aluminium chloride was supplied in an alcohol base? *(1 mark)*

3 A silicone preparation solved the problem. Silicones contain chains of silicon and oxygen atoms, with carbon atoms attached to the silicons:

$$-\underset{|}{\overset{|}{Si}}-O-\underset{\underset{\displaystyle -\underset{|}{\overset{|}{C}}-}{\overset{|}{Si}}}{}-O-\underset{|}{\overset{|}{Si}}-$$

What type of bonding is present in silicones? *(1 mark)*

4 When aluminium chloride reacts with moisture, aluminium hydroxide forms. Would you expect this to be soluble or insoluble in water? Give a reason for your answer. *(2 marks)*

5 If aluminium chloride has the formula $AlCl_3$, what would you expect the formula of aluminium hydroxide to be? *(1 mark)*

6 Write a balanced equation for the reaction between aluminium chloride and water. *(2 marks)*

7 Why do you think this article appeared on the *business* pages of the newspaper? *(2 marks)*

Guardian, 23 February 1987
(by Ian Williams)

Some people think that hydrogen might one day become an important fuel.

A herald for the age of hydrogen

BERIT Pegg-Karlsson in Polperro, Cornwall, is director of the new British-Scandinavian Association for Wind and Hydrogen Power, backed by the Pure Energy Trust. She plans to popularize in Britain the successful hydrogen 'Welgas' experiment, financed in the town of Harnosand by the Swedish steel industry, Saab and other firms.

In Harnosand, Olaf Tegstrom designed and lived in a house where the electricity came from a small computer-controlled Danish windmill in the garden. The electricity was used to electrolyse filtered water into its constituents, hydrogen and oxygen, with the hydrogen gas used for cooking, heating the house and as fuel for a Saab car.

The car is non-polluting, as the exhaust consists almost entirely of water vapour. The safe storage problem has been solved, with the gas absorbed to form a metal hydride and released as required.

Pegg-Karlsson believes that hydrogen will eventually become the world's prime provider of energy. Its energy content is three to four times higher than that of oil, and it can be produced from all known energy sources, besides being a by-product of many industrial processes. In West Berlin, thanks to government subsidies for fuels that do not cause acid rain, Daimler Benz has built a filling station where converted vehicles can be filled with hydrogen produced from town gas.

Pegg-Karlsson is enthusiastic about her Association's potential: 'It's all about positive development, caring for the Earth and taking steps towards a sustainable future society. Hydrogen power is Jules Verne's old dream come true—using water as a fuel. The technology is already available. It is largely a question of people and politicians taking brave decisions.

Guardian, 18 February 1987
(by Nicholas Albery)

1   In Harnosand, what is the kinetic energy of the wind converted into? What device is used?   *(2 marks)*

2   **(a)** In Harnosand, electricity is used to break water into its constituents. What are these constituents?   *(1 mark)*
   (b) Write a balanced chemical equation for this reaction.   *(2 marks)*
   (c) Is the reaction exothermic or endothermic?   *(1 mark)*
   (d) What would be suitable as electrodes for this process? Why?   *(2 marks)*
   (e) At which electrode would you expect hydrogen gas to be produced?   *(1 mark)*

3   Suggest a reason why the water was filtered before it was electrolysed.   *(1 mark)*

4   **(a)** Why do most fuels for cars cause pollution?   *(1 mark)*
   (b) Why is hydrogen described as non-polluting?   *(1 mark)*

5   **(a)** Why is it necessary to devise a safe storage system for hydrogen? What is the problem?   *(2 marks)*
   (b) The hydrogen gas is stored safely by being absorbed to form a metal *hydride*. An example of a metal *chloride* is NaCl. What might be an example of a metal hydride?   *(1 mark)*

6   Draw up a list of advantages that hydrogen has as a fuel.   *(3 marks)*

Read about this accident which occurred when silver was being recovered from scrap silver oxide, found in old hearing-aid batteries.

£850 000 damages and wedding plans

A MAN who became a 'prisoner in his own body' as a result of an industrial accident was awarded a record £850 000 in the High Court yesterday, and then announced plans to marry his nurse.

Graham Cook, 33, became a tetraplegic after inhaling deadly hydrogen sulphide gas in November 1982.

Left totally paralysed and unable to talk by the accident, he found his only means of communication was by use of a sophisticated computer.

It was on such a computer that Mr Cook, of Horton Road, Gloucester, asked his nurse, 35-year-old Tricia Stephenson, to marry him. She agreed to his screen proposal.

After yesterday's agreed settlement was announced in the High Court in Bristol, it was revealed the couple planned to wed later in the year when Mr Cook's divorce proceedings were completed.

They fell in love last year and Mrs Stephenson has been by his side during 12 days of court action which resulted in the record pay-out which, together with costs, could total nearly £1 million.

Mr Cook conducted his own case through his computer, using it to instruct his lawyers.

On Thursday, the Judge ruled after 10 days of hearing evidence on liability, that Berec Micro Batteries of Wildmere Road, Banbury, Oxfordshire, were to blame for the accident.

Collapsed

Mr Cook was supervising the recovery of silver from scrap silver oxide micro batteries of the type used in cameras and hearing aids.

The addition of iron sulphides was unknown to him and when he poured on nitric acid, deadly fumes were given off and he collapsed.

Mr Cook is the only worker ever known to have survived such a high dosage of hydrogen sulphide gas.

His wife Heather, who originally brought the damage action, was not in court yesterday when she was awarded £9000 for nursing damages and loss of earnings.

Mr Cook's future plans were outlined by his solicitor Stephan Allen. He said Mr Cook had left the young disabled unit at Ermine House in Gloucester for a bungalow as a temporary home. He now planned to have his own home specially built and adapted, to buy more computer equipment, to have constant medical attention and to travel extensively.

► 75 SILVER FROM OLD BATTERIES (A)

1 What *type* of reaction would turn silver oxide into silver?
(1 mark)

2 Silver oxide has the formula Ag_2O. What is the charge on a silver ion?
(1 mark)

3 **(a)** In the recovery process, nitric acid was to be added to the silver oxide. Silver nitrate, $AgNO_3$, would form, and what else?
(1 mark)

(b) Write a balanced chemical equation for the reaction between nitric acid and silver oxide. *(2 marks)*

4 One way of obtaining pure silver from silver nitrate would be by electrolysing it.

(a) On which electrode would silver be deposited? *(1 mark)*

(b) What substance would you use for this electrode? Why? *(2 marks)*

(c) In forming silver from silver nitrate in this way, does the silver lose or gain electrons? Write an equation. *(2 marks)*

(d) Draw a labelled diagram of the apparatus you would use to obtain silver by electrolysis in this way. *(3 marks)*

5 At the start of the recovery process, the silver oxide is mixed with a number of impurities. At what stage do they get left behind? *(1 mark)*

6 Suggest a different chemical method, not involving electrolysis, by which silver could be obtained from silver nitrate. *(2 marks)*

▶ 76 SILVER FROM OLD BATTERIES (B)

1 **(a)** Explain carefully why you might reasonably expect hydrogen sulphide to resemble water in its properties. *(2 marks)*

(b) What would you expect the formula of hydrogen sulphide to be? *(1 mark)*

(c) State two ways, suggested by the newspaper article, in which hydrogen sulphide does *not* resemble water. *(2 marks)*

2 **(a)** Iron sulphide has the formula FeS. Assuming FeS is ionic, what is the charge on a sulphide ion? What is the charge on an iron ion? Explain how you arrive at these charges. *(4 marks)*

(b) What, apart from hydrogen sulphide, would you expect to be formed when nitric acid, HNO_3, reacts with iron sulphide? What will be the formula of this product? *(2 marks)*

(c) Write a balanced chemical equation for the reaction between nitric acid and iron sulphide. *(2 marks)*

NUTRITION

Eggs contain significant amounts of the B vitamins riboflavin (B2) and B12 needed to ensure good general health. Vitamin D helps the body to utilize calcium which is essential for strong bones and teeth.

A SERVING = ONE SIZE 3 EGG
(RAW OR BOILED)

AVERAGE COMPOSITION	PER 57g (2oz) serving	PER 100g (3½oz)
Energy	353kJ/84kcal	619kJ/148kcal
Fat	6.2g	10.9g
of which Saturates	1.9g	3.4g
Polyunsaturates	0.7g	1.2g
Protein	7.0g	12.3g
Carbohydrate	0.2g	0.4g

MINERALS/ VITAMINS	RECOMMENDED DAILY AMOUNT	
Riboflavin (Vitamin B₂)	17%	0.5mg
Vitamin B₁₂	48%	1.7ug
Vitamin D	40%	1.8ug

THIS PACK CONTAINS 12 SERVINGS

INFORMATION

▶ 77–78 EGGS

This nutritional information appeared on a box of eggs bought from a supermarket.

▶ 77 EGGS (A)

1 Explain what is meant by a 'carbohydrate'. *(2 marks)*

2 **(a)** A chemist might represent the structure of a protein diagrammatically like this:

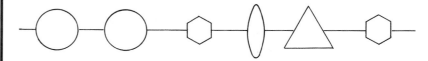

What do each of the shapes represent? *(1 mark)*

(b) Explain what happens to proteins when we digest them. *(2 marks)*

3 **(a)** What does the prefix *poly-* mean when applied to the chemistry of carbon compounds? *(1 mark)*

(b) Ethene, C_2H_4, is said to be unsaturated, but ethane, C_2H_6, is said to be saturated. Explain carefully what unsaturated/saturated mean in this case. *(2 marks)*

(c) Some of the fat present in the eggs is said to include polyunsaturates. What do you think this means? *(2 marks)*

(d) If ethene is bubbled through bromine water (or through acidified potassium manganate(VII) [permanganate]), the coloured solution turns colourless; but if ethane is used, nothing happens. What do you think would happen if the contents of an egg were shaken with bromine water or acidified potassium manganate(VII)? Explain how you arrive at your answer. *(2 marks)*

▶ 78 EGGS (B)

1 Which of the substances present in the eggs are likely to contribute most to the energy figure listed? *(2 marks)*

2 How would you attempt to show, by practical means, that the energy figure of 353 kJ per 57 g is correct? Describe what you would do, what you would measure, how you would measure it, and how you would attempt to make your results as reliable as possible. *(4 marks)*

3 The label states that vitamin D helps the body use calcium.
 (a) Why does the body need calcium? *(1 mark)*
 (b) From where would the body get this calcium? *(1 mark)*
 (c) Why is it reasonable to expect that the element strontium (atomic number 38) will behave in a very similar way to calcium? *(1 mark)*
 (d) The testing of atomic weapons may release many radioactive isotopes into the environment. Although no more radioactive than other isotopes, strontium-90 causes a particular worry. Why do you think the presence of radioactive strontium in the environment might be especially worrying? *(3 marks)*

▶ 79–80 HARD WATER

These questions refer to parts of an advertising leaflet produced by a manufacturer of water softeners.
 In answering the questions which follow, you will need to refer to the equations below.
(In equation **(iii)** the symbol St represents a complicated chain of C, H and O atoms.)

 (i) $Ca(HCO_3)_2(aq) \longrightarrow CaCO_3(s) + H_2O(l) + CO_2(g)$

 (ii) $CaCO_3(s) + H_2O(l) + CO_2(g) \longrightarrow Ca(HCO_3)_2(aq)$

 (iii) $Ca(HCO_3)_2(aq) + 2NaSt(aq) \longrightarrow CaSt_2(s) + 2NaHCO_3(aq)$

 (iv) $H_2O(l) \longrightarrow H_2O(g)$

 (v) $H_2O(g) \longrightarrow H_2O(l)$

▶ 79 HARD WATER (A)

1 Look at the water cycle as drawn.
 (a) Which of the five equations **(i)** to **(v)** best represents what is happening at **X**? *(1 mark)*
 (b) What word is used to describe this process? *(1 mark)*
 (c) Which of the five equations **(i)** to **(v)** best represents what is happening at **Y**? *(1 mark)*
 (d) What word do we use to describe this process?

(1 mark)

Turn over (question continues)

In the beginning, our water is pure and soft and gentle, but underground, deep down among the sedimentary rocks, lurk scale and scum. They dissolve in our water and are carried through the mains water pipes to our homes.
 Once inside, they cause all sorts of problems and needless expense.

2 **(a)** What is meant by a 'sedimentary rock'? *(1 mark)*
   (b) Which of the sedimentary rocks shown will cause hard water? *(1 mark)*
   (c) Explain why this type of rock causes hardness. *(1 mark)*
   (d) Which of the equations **(i)** to **(v)** best describes the formation of this hard water? *(1 mark)*

3 Water hardness can be either temporary or permanent.
   (a) What is the difference between the two sorts of hardness? *(2 marks)*
   (b) Will the hard water shown forming in the diagram be temporary or permanent? Why? *(2 marks)*

▶ 80 HARD WATER (B)

(See also page 97.)

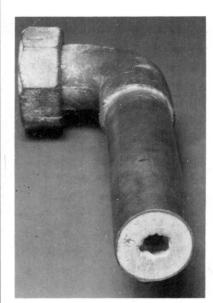

SCALE IN YOUR TANK

Wastes energy

The picture shows what expensive things scale does inside our hot water tanks. It covers the heat exchanger with a layer of limescale which makes it burn less efficiently so that you burn more fuel to heat the water.

SCALE IN YOUR PIPES

Scale gets in your pipes and slowly but surely blocks them up. Eventually you will have to replace them.

1 **(a)** What is limescale, chemically? *(1 mark)*
   (b) How does limescale form? *(1 mark)*
   (c) Which of the equations **(i)** to **(v)** on page 97 best represents the formation of limescale? *(1 mark)*
   (d) Explain how limescale in a boiler would waste energy. *(2 marks)*

SCUM IN YOUR WATER

Soap in hard water curdles to produce a sticky, unpleasant scum. Many people think this is dirt, but it isn't. Scum adheres to everything it touches including YOU and is often the cause of skin complaints and poor complexions.

WHAT IS SOFTENED WATER?

A domestic water softener removes the dissolved hardness minerals in water and reverts the water to a more natural state. Rain water is known to be gentle and soft and you will find that softened water is even more refined. It is so much nicer to wash in. Its silky texture lathers soap in abundance without creating scum.

2   **(a)** From a chemist's point of view, what is soap?
                                                    (1 mark)
   (b) What is scum?   *(1 mark)*
   (c) Which of the equations **(i)** to **(v)** on page 97 best represents the formation of scum?   *(1 mark)*
   (d) Why does scum formation waste soap?   *(1 mark)*
   (e) Apart from wasting soap, why is scum formation a nuisance?   *(1 mark)*

3   The firm that produced this advertising leaflet is selling ion exchange resins as a method of softening water.
   (a) *Either*   explain in detail how ion exchange resins work as a method of softening water;
           or   give an account of different possible methods of softening hard water.   *(5 marks)*
   (b) Suppose you had attempted to soften hard water using one of these methods. How could you check to see if it had worked?   *(2 marks)*

▶ 81 CONCRETE

Many modern buildings are made of concrete. Sometimes, small stalactites can be seen where water drips down from the roof, as on this picture taken at a school in London. The problem is not confined to schools, however, as the cutting from the *Guardian* indicates.

1   Concrete usually contains some calcium oxide, CaO, left over from its manufacture.

    (a) From what raw material would the calcium oxide have been made? *(1 mark)*

    (b) Silicon dioxide is also needed in the manufacture of concrete. What is the common source of this substance? *(1 mark)*

2   Most of the calcium oxide will have been neutralized during manufacture by the silicon dioxide, forming calcium silicate. If this is a neutralization, what is the base and what is the acid? *(1 mark)*

3   Rainwater, soaking through the concrete, gradually dissolves any calcium oxide remaining, giving calcium hydroxide solution.

    (a) Copy this equation, putting in the appropriate symbols of state:

$$CaO(\ ) + H_2O(\ ) \longrightarrow Ca(OH)_2(\ ) \quad \textit{(1 mark)}$$

    (b) What is calcium hydroxide solution better known as, in the chemistry laboratory? *(1 mark)*

    (c) Would you expect this solution to be acidic, neutral or alkaline? Why? *(1 mark)*

4   When the calcium hydroxide solution meets carbon dioxide in the air, a reaction takes place.

    (a) Copy and complete this equation for the reaction:

$$Ca(OH)_2(aq) + CO_2(g) \longrightarrow \quad \textit{(2 marks)}$$

    (b) What do you think is the chemical composition of the stalactite shown in the photograph? *(1 mark)*

5   Because of acid rain, the primitive plants known as lichens do not grow well in most towns, but they do grow well on the concrete walls of the London school. Suggest why they are able to grow on the concrete in spite of acid rain. *(1 mark)*

6   The chemistry described above, for the formation of stalactites on concrete, does not represent the way stalactites

The next show at the exhibition halls in the Barbican Centre in the City of London could well consist of the kind of stalactites and fungus which would do justice to a 1960s system-built housing block. A report to be presented to the City's common council tomorrow warns that such interesting growths are already spreading round the ceilings and £2.2 million is needed to put it right. Since the halls are a nice little earner, the idea is to keep them open during repairs.

Guardian, 18 February 1987

form in caves in limestone areas. Here, their formation may be described by this equation:

$$Ca(HCO_3)_2(aq) \longrightarrow CaCO_3(s) + H_2O(l) + CO_2(g)$$

With the help of this equation, explain how stalactites form in limestone caves. *(4 marks)*

▶ 82–83   THALLIUM PESTICIDE POLLUTION

The following story appeared in the *Observer*.

Sugar alert after hundreds die from pesticide

EXTRA checks on food imports to Britain from Guyana have been ordered as evidence emerges of a major pesticide pollution problem in the South American republic.

Though the Guyanese regime is seeking to minimize the affair, British medical experts say several hundred people have already died from poisoning by thallium, a highly toxic metal used as a pesticide.

Thallium, in the form of thallium sulphate, was used in Guyana until January to keep down cane rats on sugar plantations.

Dr John Henry of Guy's Hospital in London, an expert on poisons who has been helping the Guyanese authorities, says a large proportion of Guyana's population of 800 000 could have been affected by thallium. Less than one gram of thallium sulphate can be a lethal dose, producing delirium, coma, convulsions and haemorrhage.

The poison, whose use has been outlawed in Britain and other developed countries for more than 20 years, was employed on the plantations of Guysuco, the Guyana state sugar corporation, until last January despite urgent warnings last year. Guysuco has 3 000 lbs of the poison in store.

In one Guyanese hospital last year, 14 out of 22 people treated for thallium poisoning died.

Last April, after a dinner party for 15 people at which thallium-affected food was served, five people died and the survivors were found to have swallowed near-lethal doses of the substance.

Scenes of near panic have taken place in Georgetown, the Guyanese capital, as crowds descended on the newly-opened Thallium Treatment Centre at the city's government hospital.

Emergency supplies of Prussian blue, a powder used to make ink and the main antidote to thallium, have been flown out to Guyana and the National Poisons Information Centre in London has been swamped by appeals from individual Guyanese doctors and patients.

Tate and Lyle which imports the bulk of Guyanese sugar into Britain confirmed it was analyzing all Guyanese sugar imported since 1985. The company says it has found no evidence of it in its supplies. The Agriculture Ministry said yesterday it was satisfied with the company's checks but was extending monitoring to all agricultural products imported from Guyana.

Tate and Lyle said it was not yet satisfied any deaths had occurred in Guyana from thallium poisoning.

Observer, 22 March 1987

▶ 82   THALLIUM PESTICIDE POLLUTION (A)

1   Thallium sulphate was used as a pesticide on the sugar plantations.

(a) What job was it doing? *(1 mark)*

(b) Most pesticides are dangerous. Why do we use them? *(2 marks)*

2   Why do you think this pesticide was being used in Guyana, 20 years after it was banned in Britain? *(2 marks)*

3   The company importing sugar into Britain from Guyana 'said it was not yet satisfied any deaths had occurred in Guyana from thallium poisoning'. What evidence would it be necessary to collect in order to prove that thallium poisoning had occurred? *(2 marks)*

▶ 83 THALLIUM PESTICIDE POLLUTION (B)

See the report on page 101.

1 The symbol for thallium is Tl. Use the periodic table at the back of this book to identify which Group thallium is found in.
(1 mark)

2 Why might you expect thallium to form Tl^{3+} ions? *(1 mark)*

3 Although it does form Tl^{3+} ions, it is more common as Tl^+, e.g. in the thallium sulphate referred to in the newspaper story. If sulphate ions are SO_4^{2-} what is the formula for thallium sulphate? *(1 mark)*

4 What is the mass of 1 mole of thallium sulphate? (Relative atomic masses are given at the end of this book.) *(1 mark)*

5 How many moles of thallium sulphate are in 1 g, the fatal dose? *(1 mark)*

6 The main antidote to thallium poisoning is said to be Prussian blue, $K^+Fe^{2+}Fe^{3+}(CN^-)_6$ (or $KFe_2(CN)_6$). A possible way in which this antidote could work would be for the thallium sulphate to react forming insoluble $Tl^+Fe^{2+}Fe^{3+}(CN^-)_6$ (or $TlFe_2(CN)_6$) together with potassium sulphate. Write a balanced chemical equation for this reaction. *(3 marks)*

▶ 84–87 CHERNOBYL

In April 1986 the nuclear reactor at Chernobyl, in the Soviet Union, exploded. At the time, reasons—and the likely effects—were not well understood, and it was many months before a clear picture emerged. Questions 84 to 87 are based on press reports and letters published at the time, and reflect the great confusion on the part of scientists and public alike.

▶ 84 CHERNOBYL (A)

The drawing on the next page, published in the *Observer* on 4 May, 1986, shows how that newspaper thought the accident might have happened (although it was later found not to be so).

1 Zircaloy is an alloy composed mainly of the element zirconium. What is meant by the term 'alloy'? *(1 mark)*

2 Where is zirconium in the periodic table? In general terms, what sort of properties will it have? *(4 marks)*

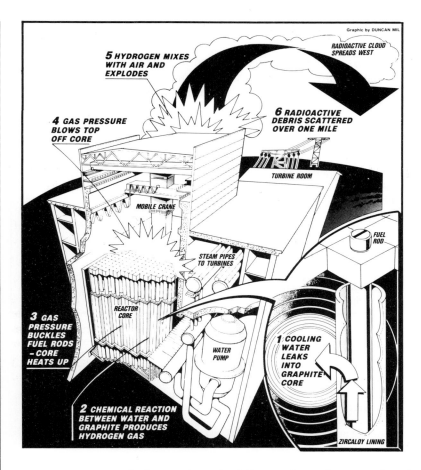

Graphic by DUNCAN MIL

5 HYDROGEN MIXES WITH AIR AND EXPLODES

RADIOACTIVE CLOUD SPREADS WEST

4 GAS PRESSURE BLOWS TOP OFF CORE

6 RADIOACTIVE DEBRIS SCATTERED OVER ONE MILE

TURBINE ROOM

MOBILE CRANE

FUEL ROD

STEAM PIPES TO TURBINES

REACTOR CORE

3 GAS PRESSURE BUCKLES FUEL RODS – CORE HEATS UP

1 COOLING WATER LEAKS INTO GRAPHITE CORE

WATER PUMP

2 CHEMICAL REACTION BETWEEN WATER AND GRAPHITE PRODUCES HYDROGEN GAS

ZIRCALOY LINING

3 Water to cool the nuclear fuel flows through pipes lined with zircaloy. What does this tell you about its position in the reactivity series? *(1 mark)*

4 When the pressurized water leaks out of the zircaloy pipes, it turns at once to steam. Why? *(1 mark)*

5 What is graphite? *(1 mark)*

6 When steam comes into contact with hot graphite, hydrogen is formed.
    (a) What else would you expect to be formed? *(1 mark)*
    (b) Write an equation for this reaction. *(2 marks)*
    (c) When graphite reacts with steam in this way, there is a large increase in the volume of gas. Why? *(1 mark)*
    (d) What is oxidized in this reaction? *(1 mark)*

7 Why is the formation of hydrogen a problem? *(1 mark)*

Site of accident at Chernobyl nuclear power plant. Cloud of radioactivity reported over Sweden, Finland and Denmark.

As a result of the accident at Chernobyl (see page 102), a mixture of various radioactive isotopes escaped from the reactor and spread across the world, getting into rainwater, plants and food. Read the newspaper reports and letters which appeared at the time.

It has been assumed that Sweden bore the brunt of the initial fallout cloud, but measurements of radioactivity in water, milk and vegetables in West Germany, Britain and Poland are now approaching emergency reference levels.

Austria banned the sale of leaf vegetables, including lettuce and cabbage, as well as cauliflower, beans, peas and tomatoes and barred their import from Bulgaria, Italy, Yugoslavia, Poland, Romania, Czechoslovakia, the Soviet Union and Hungary, after finding a high level of radiation.

Milk in Bavaria is reported to contain five times as much iodine-131 as currently in Britain. The figure of over 1 000 Becquerels (the standard unit of measurement for radioactivity) is well above the level which in Britain would require action to be taken.

Guardian, 6 May 1986

By yesterday, radiation levels in Scandinavia, which increased by up to six times the natural background level (and much more, apparently, where rain fell) had begun to fall as the original radiation cloud drifted back across the Baltic.

Public concern was still very much there.

Guardian, 7 May 1986

Earlier reports that there was a spontaneous evacuation from Minsk, several hundred miles to the north, were not substantiated in Kiev, with a population of 2.5 million and drawing its water from the river which feeds the lake at Chernobyl about 60 miles away. The situation was reported apparently normal.

While the British embassy in Moscow was warning the 70 or so British exchange students in Kiev to drink only boiled water, Intourist, the Soviet tourist agency, made no immediate move to discourage further visitors.

Guardian, 7 May 1986

Sir,—Now that the keening chorus of the self-appointed guardians of our good—Greenpeace, CND, Sana, etc.—who seem to have automatic right of first access to your columns have had their say, can we drop the hysteria and hyperbole and attempt to return to some sort of sense of proportion in connection with the Chernobyl accident.

An accident in which two people died—do you know any different?—is a small accident, not Armageddon. As an example of the hysteria and hyperbole, the letter (May 3) from L. Williams of the Green Party will serve.

The world did not come to an end with the Windscale fire in 1957; Three Mile Island in retrospect, is remarkable for all the things which did not happen, in spite of the mistakes made by the operators of the plant. Your correspondent even has to bring in a hypothetical worst case, and a sodium fire in a nonexistent power station, to make the usual point: 'all nuclear processes bad, all alternatives better.'

This is nonsense. There are no risk-free industrial processes. We kill, in this country alone, 10 times as many every day, as have died at Chernobyl. Coal mining and oil extraction are many times as hazardous as nuclear power generation.

Why then, do you and your correspondents treat the nuclear industry as something uniquely different and uniquely evil? Part of the reason is the conflation of nuclear power with atomic weapons. Certainly the connection exists, but it is neither greater nor less than that between conventional chemistry and conventional explosives.

Guardian Letters, 8 May 1986

1 Why do you think that the increase in radioactivity was detected first in Sweden, Finland and Denmark? *(2 marks)*

2 A school in Yorkshire featured on television because it was apparently the only place in the country which was continuously monitoring radiation levels in the air during the days following the accident. What equipment would the school have used for this? *(2 marks)*

3 If rainwater, and hence drinking water, was contaminated with radioactive isotopes, do you think the advice issued by the British embassy in Moscow to drink only boiled water was very helpful? Explain your reasons carefully. *(2 marks)*

4 Explain carefully how radiation would have got into vegetables and milk. *(2 marks)*

5 Do you agree with the writer of the letter to the *Guardian*? Write a letter to the newspaper about nuclear power, either supporting or opposing this view. *(4 marks)*

▶ **86 CHERNOBYL (C)**

One of the main isotopes which was dispersed as a result of the accident at Chernobyl (see page 102) was iodine-131. ^{131}I is a β-emitter, with a half-life of 8 days.

1 Explain the meaning of the number 131 in ^{131}I. *(1 mark)*

2 Use the periodic table (printed at the back of this book) to work out what iodine-131 decays to. *(2 marks)*

3 1 Becquerel = 1 radioactive disintegration/second. If a litre of milk has an activity of 200 Bq now, and this is due entirely to iodine-131, what will the activity be in 8 days time? What will it be in 16 days from now? *(2 marks)*

4 Read this extract. Do you think this newspaper was correct in saying that the problem will be resolved in 2 to 3 weeks? Explain your reasons carefully. *(2 marks)*

> The radioactivity from Chernobyl now seems to be falling in significant amounts wherever rainfall is high, and in West Germany, some spinach plants have been found to contain over 10 times the permitted level. General levels are still below the risk standard.
>
> The majority of the radioactivity is still iodine-131, which has a short life. In another two or three weeks, the problems may be substantially resolved provided there are no further releases.

Guardian, 6 May 1986

Turn over (question continues)

5 Food would inevitably become contaminated with iodine-131. Read the two letters which appeared in the *Guardian* on 8 May 1986.

Sir,—Because of a planned visit to Austria and the reported radioactive contamination of food there, I asked the young lady serving at the counter of a large branch of a retail pharmaceutical chemist for potassium iodide tablets suitable for children aged between five and eight years.

She disappeared to consult her colleagues, but soon returned to say that the demand had been so great they had no more left. However they would provide me with a solution of potassium iodide which was just as effective. Would I return in 15 minutes so that the pharmacist could make up the prescription?

Later the pharmacist herself told me that she could not provide me with the potassium iodide because there was nothing in their reference texts which defined the dose; nor had they received any information from the Government as to the appropriate doses either for children or adults.

However she had most kindly rung up the Austrian Embassy and inquired about the precautions they were recommending. They knew nothing about the recommended doses of potassium iodide, but suggested that fresh vegetables should be avoided or carefully washed.

One wonders what the National Radiological Protection Board and the Ministry of Health are for. Yours sincerely,

Peter Thonemann.
University College of Swansea.

Sir,—Your or your correspondents' case isn't helped by the total ignorance of the subject matter displayed in your reporting of some of the issues. On page five beside a picture of a child being given something to drink to protect it from radiation, you report the substance as iodine (twice) and as sodium iodine (sic) once. If you mean the first, you may well have killed more children than Chernobyl. Yours, etc,

Alex Milne.

Guardian, 8 May 1986

Why was the writer of the first letter so keen to obtain tablets of potassium iodide? What effect would it have if someone was to swallow relatively large doses of non-radioactive iodide?
(2 marks)

6 Why does the writer of the second letter suggest that giving children iodine could harm them? What chemical point was he trying to make?
(3 marks)

Ten months after Chernobyl (see page 102), there were still problems, as these extracts from an article about sheep farmers in the Lake District indicate.

Sheep still too hot to handle

The Chernobyl clouds have drifted away from most of our lives—but they continue to hang heavily over the hill farmers of the Lake District. A hundred and fifty of them still work in areas where they are banned from moving their sheep because of the continuing high levels of caesium-137. Many more are still suffering financial hardship. Charles Searle reports on their anger with the men from the Ministry.

Today, the issues are still alive. Farmers are still out of pocket and angry. Their dissatisfaction began with the way they were kept in the dark about the contamination of their livestock and the disruption this would cause to their livelihoods. The first inkling most of them had that there was a problem came on June 20, when Michael Jopling announced in the Commons that he was placing a ban on the movement and sale of all sheep on 1 500 farms in south-west Cumbria and North Wales. What he failed to tell MPs was that he had been contemplating such a course of action for the previous six weeks.

Within days of the fall out from Chernobyl drifting over Britain at the beginning of May, information on the composition and distribution of the radioactive deposits started to reach Jopling's Ministry. A national sample of grassland and vegetation by the Institute of Terrestrial Ecology pinpointed the upland areas as those most severely contaminated by the long lived caesium-137. All the samples from Cumbria exceeded the 'action level' suggested by the National Radiological Protection Board for removing livestock from grazing out of doors.

The Ministry of Agriculture refused to follow the Board's advice, mainly because hill farms do not have the buildings to accommodate all their livestock; but it did start testing slaughtered lambs for radio-caesium. By mid-May the first results from these tests showed that the amounts of caesium-137 in Cumbrian lambs were well above the 1 000 Becquerels per kilo limit approved that month by the EEC as the level at which restrictions should come into force. Yet Jopling was still claiming at the end of the month that 'we have always been a long way from the stage when we need to contemplate any sort of restriction.'

While Roger Ward continues to press the Ministry to reconsider the cases of those farmers debarred from compensation, the 150 Cumbrian farmers whose land is still within the restricted area face the coming spring with little hope of relief. Although readings for caesium-137 in the uplands register a drop to 25–30% of the levels immediately after Chernobyl, these farmers will have yet another crop of contaminated lambs.

Guardian, 7 March 1987

1 Use the data in the periodic table at the end of this book to state the number of protons, neutrons and electrons in an atom of caesium-137. *(3 marks)*

2 The daughter product of caesium-137 is barium-137. Is caesium-137 an α- or a β-emitter? Explain your reasoning. *(1 mark)*

3 The article describes caesium-137 as long-lived. Explain what this means. (Caesium-137's half-life is 30 years.) *(2 marks)*

4 The article suggests that the activity will drop to 25% of its original value within 10 months. Would you have expected this with a half-life of 30 years? Explain your answer. *(2 marks)*

5 What common element would you expect to resemble caesium chemically? Give a reason for your choice. *(2 marks)*

6 Suggest the route by which caesium-137 gets from the rain into Cumbrian lambs. *(2 marks)*

7 Suppose you were a sheep farmer in Cumbria. Write a letter to the newspaper, explaining your views on nuclear power. *(4 marks)*

► 88–90 URANIUM HEXAFLUORIDE

Questions 88 to 90 relate to this newspaper report of a shipping accident.

Guardian, 27 August 1984

Shipping in Channel is warned to avoid any contact with wreckage
Uranium gas tanks sank with freighter

The French cargo ship which sunk in the Channel on Saturday after a collision with a ferry was carrying 450 tons of radioactive and highly explosive material.

Alarm among the 1 200 passengers and crew of the ferry, the Olau Britannia, that they may have been contaminated was discounted by the ferry company last night.

They said that the French Navy had investigated the waters round the wreck off Ostend, and said that there was no radioactive leak. Independent searches aboard the damaged ferry had found no contamination.

But the cargo of uranium hexaflouride now in 60 feet of water is highly corrosive, and will explode violently in contact with sea water.

Vessels using the busy shipping lanes where the 4 200-ton ship sank have been warned not to handle any wreckage found in the area, and two Belgian patrol boats are guarding the wreck.

After the collision in which the ferry hit the French vessel, the Mont-Louis, amidships, tugs were called to pull them apart. They remained locked together for some hours, but when they were separated the French ship sank immediately.

The owners said last night that they believed the cargo was undamaged. Experts said that the chemical is used as a gas, but at normal temperatures is a solid. It is more dangerous as an explosive chemical than a source of radioactivity. It was like having a chemical bomb on the sea bed.

This conflicts with a statement issued by the ship owners, who said that the radioactivity would be absorbed into the environment. 'Even if a leak were to develop, the radioactive material would quickly be diluted by the seawater.'

Yesterday the French owners of the ship, Compagnie Generale Maritime, telexed Belgian coastguards at Ostend to warn them that the cargo contained radioactive material. Belgian coastguards warned all shipping of the wreck, and said that its cargo contained radioactive waste partly packed in yellow drums, marked IMCO 7.

The message read: 'Mariners are advised to avoid handling these goods. If picked up accidentally, please contact Ostend pilotage.' IMCO 7 is an international mark used by the International Maritime Organization to denote radioactive cargoes. Yellow is used for the two most dangerous of a possible three categories of radioactive strength.

The French ship had sailed from Le Havre on Thursday and was due to arrive at the Soviet port of Riga today. The company regularly carries enriched and impoverished uranium between Russia and France in an exchange agreement to supply nuclear reactors in both countries. The company normally uses the Mont-Louis's sister ship, the Borodine, which is currently undergoing maintenance at Le Havre.

The maritime branch of the French Democratic Labour Federation said that before the ship sailed the crew

had demanded extra payment for handling radioactive cargo. The company refused, but issued each crew member with a gauge showing how much radioactivity he was receiving.

The environmental group Greenpeace, whose statement issued in Paris broke the news of the ship's radioactive cargo, said that it was appealing to transport unions not to handle nuclear cargo. The National Union of Seamen and other transport unions have already refused to handle nuclear waste to be dumped at sea.

Last December the Sealink-owned ship, Speedlink Vanguard, which regularly carries uranium and nuclear waste to and from the Continent, was in collision with another ferry. The Sealink ship was not carrying nuclear waste at the time.

This latest incident will intensify a campaign being mounted in France to prevent a shipment of 500 lbs of plutonium from being sent to Japan.

Anthony Tucker adds: Uranium hexafluoride in its solid form is used in the uranium enrichment process in the creation of material for nuclear fuels or for nuclear weapons.

It is normally transported in containers designed to withstand accidental impact, and when carried at sea should be in extra strong containers designed to withstand crushing, which could occur at great depths under the sea.

If sea water were to leak in, the strong containers would simply become the outer casings of chemical bombs.

▶ 88 URANIUM HEXAFLUORIDE (A)

1 The accident involved the chemical uranium hexafluoride. According to one textbook, 'Uranium hexafluoride sublimes at 56 °C'. Is the newspaper correct to say in the headline, 'Uranium gas tanks sank...'? Explain your answer. *(2 marks)*

2 Would you expect uranium hexafluoride to be ionic or covalent? Give a reason. *(2 marks)*

3 The uranium hexafluoride was stored in mild steel cylinders, which corrode in sea water at a rate of about 0.16 mm per year. The steel was about 16 mm thick. About how long would you expect it to take before the cylinders begin to leak? *(1 mark)*

4 Uranium hexafluoride reacts readily with water. Would you expect this reaction to be exothermic or endothermic? *(1 mark)*

5 When uranium hexafluoride, UF_6, reacts with water, it forms uranyl fluoride, UO_2F_2, and hydrogen fluoride, HF. Write a balanced chemical equation for this reaction. *(2 marks)*

6 Uranyl fluoride is described in one book as ionic, $UO_2^{2+}(F^-)_2$. Predict whether it will be a gas, liquid, or solid at room temperature and pressure, giving a reason for your prediction. *(2 marks)*

7 Why might you expect hydrogen fluoride to have similar properties to hydrogen chloride? *(1 mark)*

8 The newspaper report talks about 'the cargo of uranium hexaflouride'. What is wrong with this statement? *(1 mark)*

▶ 89 URANIUM HEXAFLUORIDE (B)

1 The report states that the French Navy found no evidence of a radioactive leak. What instrument would they use to look for any such leak? *(1 mark)*

2 **(a)** Uranium hexafluoride is made from natural uranium, which is a mixture of ^{235}U and ^{238}U. What word is used to describe uranium-235 and uranium-238? *(1 mark)*
(b) Draw up a table to show the numbers of protons, neutrons and electrons in atoms of uranium-235 and uranium-238. (You may use the periodic table at the end of this book.) *(3 marks)*

3 **(a)** What is the mass of 1 mole of $^{235}UF_6$? (Relative atomic masses are given on the periodic table at the end of this book). *(1 mark)*

(b) What mass of fluorine is required to convert 235 g uranium-235 into uranium hexafluoride? *(2 marks)*

(c) $^{235}UF_6$ is separated from $^{238}UF_6$ by diffusion. What difference between $^{235}UF_6$ and $^{238}UF_6$ allows them to be separated in this way? *(1 mark)*

4 **(a)** Uranium-235 is an α-emitter. Explain what this means. *(1 mark)*

(b) Write an equation which shows the α-decay of uranium-235. (You may find the periodic table at the end of the book useful.) *(2 marks)*

5 **(a)** The half-life of uranium-235 is 713 000 000 years. Explain what this means. *(1 mark)*

(b) The half-life of uranium-238 is 4 510 000 000 years. If you had equal amounts of uranium-235 and uranium-238, which would be the more radioactive? Explain how you arrive at your answer. *(2 marks)*

▶ 90 URANIUM HEXAFLUORIDE (C)

Uranium hexafluoride is used to make fuel for nuclear power stations, and accidents like that described on page 108 are one of the hazards of nuclear power. On the other hand, coal and oil fired power stations can result in the production of acid rain. Write a letter to a newspaper, setting out the pros and cons of nuclear power. *(8 marks)*

▶ 91 STATUE OF EROS

This well-known statue, in London's Piccadilly Circus, has been in place for about a hundred years. It is made of aluminium, and has suffered virtually no damage from corrosion.

1 **(a)** What conclusion can you draw from this absence of corrosion? *(1 mark)*

  (b) Does this conclusion surprise you, in view of the position of aluminium in the reactivity series? Explain your answer. *(2 marks)*

2 Aluminium is often used for making kettles and cooking pans.

  (a) State two properties which make aluminium a good choice for this purpose *(2 marks)*

  (b) Why isn't the aluminium attacked by boiling water, or by food put into the pans for cooking? *(2 marks)*

3 State two further important uses for aluminium. *(2 marks)*

4 Around 1850, aluminium cost about £15 per kilogram— more than the cost of gold in those days! Why do you think aluminium was so expensive then, and why is it much cheaper now? *(2 marks)*

5 **(a)** From what ore is aluminium obtained today? *(1 mark)*

  (b) Why is it difficult to extract aluminium from this ore? *(2 marks)*

  (c) Outline the method by which aluminium is obtained from this ore nowadays. *(4 marks)*

▶ 92–94 FERTILIZERS

Compare the two fertilizer bags shown in the photographs.

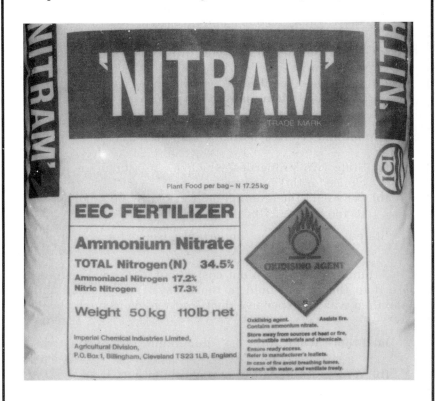

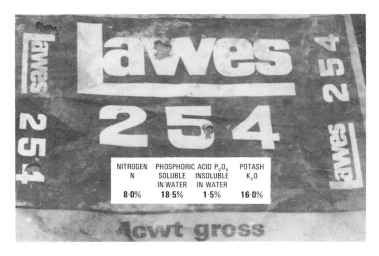

NITROGEN N	PHOSPHORIC ACID P_2O_5 SOLUBLE IN WATER	INSOLUBLE IN WATER	POTASH K_2O
8·0%	18·5%	1·5%	16·0%

► 92 FERTILIZERS (A)

1 **(a)** Why do we use fertilizers? *(1 mark)*
  (b) Why has the amount of fertilizer used increased greatly
    in recent years? *(2 marks)*

2 Lawes 254 would be described as an 'NPK fertilizer'.
  (a) What do these letters stand for? *(3 marks)*
  (b) Why are NPK fertilizers particularly useful? *(1 mark)*

3 Despite what the bag says, Lawes 254 does *not* contain
'potash K_2O'—this is just a rather old-fashioned way of letting
farmers know how much potassium is present.
  (a) Why would it be undesirable to put potassium oxide,
    K_2O, directly on the soil? *(1 mark)*
  (b) Potassium may be included in fertilizers either in the
    form of potassium sulphate, or as potassium chloride.
    How would you test this fertilizer to see which it
    contained, or to see if it contained both? *(4 marks)*
  (c) Crops grown on a heavy clay soil do not need a
    potassium fertilizer. Suggest why not. *(1 mark)*

4 Describe the problems which can arise from using too much
fertilizer. *(4 marks)*

► 93 FERTILIZERS (B)

1 Look at the bag of ICI Nitram fertilizer. Ammonium nitrate
has the formula NH_4NO_3.
  (a) Why does the bag have a warning sign on it? *(1 mark)*
  (b) What is meant when the bag refers to 'ammoniacal
    nitrogen' and 'nitric nitrogen'? *(1 mark)*
  (c) If the bag contained pure ammonium nitrate, what
    percentage of the mass would be nitrogen? (Relative
    atomic masses are given on the periodic table at the end
    of the book.) *(2 marks)*
  (d) What mass of ammonia is needed in order to make 50 kg
    ammonium nitrate? *(2 marks)*
  (e) Why does the bag say, 'Plant Food per bag—N
    17.25 kg'? *(1 mark)*

Turn over (question continues)

2 This flow diagram illustrates how ammonium nitrate is manufactured.

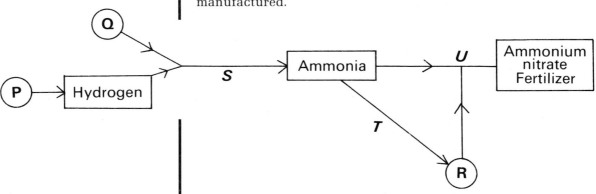

(a) What are the raw materials **P** and **Q**? *(2 marks)*
(b) What is the name given to process **S**? *(1 mark)*
(c) What is the intermediate **R**? *(1 mark)*
(d) What *type* of reactions are **T** and **U**? *(2 marks)*

3 Suppose you wished to decide which of Lawes 254 and ICI Nitram was best for growing beans. How would you carry out your investigation? What would you do, what would you look for, and how would you interpret your results? *(4 marks)*

▶ 94 FERTILIZERS (C)

The bag of Lawes 254, shown on page 112, holds 1 cwt, which is almost exactly 50 kg.

1 As stated in question 91, the fertilizer does not actually contain K_2O.
(a) If there *was* 16 % K_2O, what mass would there be in this bag? *(1 mark)*
(b) If all the potassium is, in fact, present as potassium sulphate, K_2SO_4, what mass of potassium sulphate must there be in order to achieve the same amount of potassium as 16% K_2O? (Relative atomic masses are given on the periodic table at the end of the book.) *(2 marks)*

2 Similarly, Lawes 254 does *not* contain phosphoric acid, which, in any case, is *not* P_2O_5!

    (a) What is the name of P_2O_5?   *(1 mark)*

    (b) The main source of phosphorus for fertilizers is phosphatic rock from Africa, $Ca_3(PO_4)_2$. This is almost insoluble in water. Why is that a disadvantage in a fertilizer?   *(1 mark)*

    (c) Most phosphatic rock is converted into the more soluble calcium superphosphate, by reaction with sulphuric acid.

$$Ca_3(PO_4)_2 + 2H_2SO_4 \longrightarrow Ca(H_2PO_4)_2 + 2CaSO_4$$

    The bag of Lawes 254 will contain about 15 kg of calcium superphosphate. What mass of phosphatic rock will have been used to make it?   *(2 marks)*

    (d) What mass of sulphuric acid would have to be used to make 15 kg of superphosphate?   *(2 marks)*

3 The bag of Lawes 254 contains 8.0 % nitrogen, or about 4 kg. Possible nitrogenous fertilizers include ammonium sulphate, ammonium nitrate, and urea. Copy and complete the following table, in order to work out how many kg of each of these fertilizers you would have to use in order to have 4 kg of nitrogen in the bag.

Fertilizer	Formula	Mass of 1 mol	How much fertilizer to obtain 4 kg nitrogen?
Ammonium sulphate Ammonium nitrate Urea	$(NH_4)_2SO_4$ NH_4NO_3 $CO(NH_2)_2$		

        (6 marks)

APPENDICES ▶

The periodic table

Group 1	Group 2											Group 3	Group 4	Group 5	Group 6	Group 7	Group 0
1.0 H 1 Hydrogen																	4.0 He 2 Helium
6.9 Li 3 Lithium	9.0 Be 4 Beryllium											10.8 B 5 Boron	12.0 C 6 Carbon	14.0 N 7 Nitrogen	16.0 O 8 Oxygen	19.0 F 9 Fluorine	20.2 Ne 10 Neon
23.0 Na 11 Sodium	24.3 Mg 12 Magnesium											27.0 Al 13 Aluminium	28.1 Si 14 Silicon	31.0 P 15 Phosphorus	32.1 S 16 Sulphur	35.5 Cl 17 Chlorine	39.9 Ar 18 Argon
39.1 K 19 Potassium	40.1 Ca 20 Calcium	45.0 Sc 21 Scandium	47.9 Ti 22 Titanium	50.9 V 23 Vanadium	52.0 Cr 24 Chromium	54.9 Mn 25 Manganese	55.9 Fe 26 Iron	58.9 Co 27 Cobalt	58.7 Ni 28 Nickel	63.5 Cu 29 Copper	65.4 Zn 30 Zinc	69.7 Ga 31 Gallium	72.6 Ge 32 Germanium	74.9 As 33 Arsenic	79.0 Se 34 Selenium	79.9 Br 35 Bromine	83.8 Kr 36 Krypton
85.5 Rb 37 Rubidium	87.6 Sr 38 Strontium	88.9 Y 39 Yttrium	91.2 Zr 40 Zirconium	92.9 Nb 41 Niobium	95.9 Mo 42 Molybdenum	99 Tc 43 Technetium	101.1 Ru 44 Ruthenium	102.9 Rh 45 Rhodium	106.4 Pd 46 Palladium	107.9 Ag 47 Silver	112.4 Cd 48 Cadmium	114.8 In 49 Indium	118.7 Sn 50 Tin	121.8 Sb 51 Antimony	127.6 Te 52 Tellurium	126.9 I 53 Iodine	131.3 Xe 54 Xenon
132.9 Cs 55 Caesium	137.3 Ba 56 Barium	138.9 La 57 Lanthanum ▼▼	178.5 Hf 72 Hafnium	181.0 Ta 73 Tantalum	183.9 W 74 Tungsten	186.2 Re 75 Rhenium	190.2 Os 76 Osmium	192.2 Ir 77 Iridium	195.1 Pt 78 Platinum	197.0 Au 79 Gold	200.6 Hg 80 Mercury	204.4 Tl 81 Thallium	207.2 Pb 82 Lead	209.0 Bi 83 Bismuth	210 Po 84 Polonium	210 At 85 Astatine	222 Rn 86 Radon
223 Fr 87 Francium	226 Ra 88 Radium	227 Ac 89 Actinium ▼▼	261 Unq 104 Unnilquadium	262 Unp 105 Unnilpentium	263 Unh 106 Unnilhexium												

Key

Relative atomic mass	
Symbol	
Atomic number	
Name	

▼ Lanthanoid elements
▼ Actinoid elements

APPENDIX 2

► SERIAL NUMBERS FOR FOOD ADDITIVES ('E' NUMBERS)

The following serial numbers for food additives may be used in the ingredients lists on food labels as alternatives to their names.

COLOURS

E100	Curcumin
E101	Riboflavin **(Lactoflavin)**
101(a)	Riboflavin-5'-phosphate
E102	Tartrazine
E104	Quinoline Yellow
107	Yellow 2G
E110	Sunset Yellow FCF **(Orange Yellow S)**
E120	Cochineal **(Carmine of Cochineal or Carminic acid)**
E122	Carmoisine **(Azorubine)**
E123	Amaranth
E124	Ponceau 4R **(Cochineal Red A)**
E127	Erythrosine BS
128	Red 2G
E131	Patent Blue V
E132	Indigo Carmine **(Indigotine)**
133	Brilliant Blue FCF
E140	Chlorophyll
E141	Copper complexes of chlorophyll and chlorophyllins
E142	Green S **(Acid Brilliant Green BS or Lissamine Green)**
E150	Caramel
E151	Black PN **(Brilliant Black BN)**
E153	Carbon Black **(Vegetable Carbon)**
154	Brown FK
155	Brown HT **(Chocolate Brown HT)**
E160(a)	alpha-carotene, beta-carotene, gamma-carotene
E160(b)	annatto, bixin, norbixin
E160(c)	capsanthin **(Capsorubin)**
E160(d)	lycopene
E160(e)	beta-apo-8'-carotenal (C_{30})
E160(f)	ethyl ester of beta-apo-8'-carotenoic acid (C_{30})
E161(a)	Flavoxanthin
E161(b)	Lutein
E161(c)	Cryptoxanthin
E161(d)	Rubixanthin
E161(e)	Violaxanthin
E161(f)	Rhodoxanthin
E161(g)	Canthaxanthin
E162	Beetroot Red **(Betanin)**
E163	Anthocyanins
E170	Calcium carbonate
E171	Titanium dioxide
E172	Iron oxides, iron hydroxides
E173	Aluminium
E174	Silver
E175	Gold
E180	Pigment Rubine **(Lithol Rubine BK)**

PRESERVATIVES

E200	Sorbic acid
E201	Sodium sorbate
E202	Potassium sorbate
E203	Calcium sorbate
E210	Benzoic acid
E211	Sodium benzoate
E212	Potassium benzoate
E213	Calcium benzoate
E214	Ethyl 4-hydroxybenzoate **(Ethyl *para*-hydroxybenzoate)**
E215	Ethyl 4-hydroxybenzoate, sodium salt **(Sodium ethyl *para*-hydroxybenzoate)**
E216	Propyl 4-hydroxybenzoate **(Propyl *para*-hydroxybenzoate)**
E217	Propyl 4-hydroxybenzoate, sodium salt **(Sodium propyl *para*-hydroxybenzoate)**
E218	Methyl 4-hydroxybenzoate **(Methyl *para*-hydroxybenzoate)**
E219	Methyl 4-hydroxybenzoate, sodium salt **(Sodium methyl *para*-hydroxybenzoate)**
E220	Sulphur dioxide
E221	Sodium sulphite
E222	Sodium hydrogen sulphite **(Sodium bisulphite)**
E223	Sodium metabisulphite
E224	Potassium metabisulphite
E226	Calcium sulphite
E227	Calcium hydrogen sulphite **(Calcium bisulphite)**
E230	Biphenyl **(Diphenyl)**

E231	2-Hydroxybiphenyl **(Orthophenylphenol)**	E331	Sodium dihydrogen citrate **(*mono*Sodium citrate)**, *di*Sodium citrate, *tri*Sodium citrate
E232	Sodium biphenyl-2-yl oxide **(Sodium orthophenylphenate)**	E332	Potassium dihydrogen citrate **(*mono*Potassium citrate)**, *tri*Potassium citrate
E233	2-(Thiazol-4-yl) benzimidazole **(Thiabendazole)**	E333	*mono*Calcium citrate, *di*Calcium citrate, *tri*Calcium citrate
234	Nisin	E334	L-(+)-Tartaric acid
E239	Hexamine **(Hexamethylenetetramine)**	E335	*mono*Sodium L-(+)-tartrate, *di*Sodium L-(+)-tartrate
E249	Potassium nitrite	E336	*mono*Potassium L-(+)-tartrate **(Cream of tartar)**, *di*Potassium L-(+)-tartrate
E250	Sodium nitrite		
E251	Sodium nitrate	E337	Potassium sodium L-(+)-tartrate
E252	Potassium nitrate		
E260	Acetic acid	E338	Orthophosphoric acid **(Phosphoric acid)**
E261	Potassium acetate	E339	Sodium dihydrogen orthophosphate, *di*Sodium hydrogen orthophosphate, *tri*Sodium orthophosphate
E262	Sodium hydrogen diacetate		
262	Sodium acetate		
E263	Calcium acetate		
E270	Lactic acid	E340	Potassium dihydrogen orthophosphate, *di*Potassium hydrogen orthophosphate, *tri*Potassium orthophosphate
E280	Propionic acid		
E281	Sodium propionate		
E282	Calcium propionate		
E283	Potassium propionate		
E290	Carbon dioxide	E341	Calcium tetrahydrogen diorthophosphate, Calcium hydrogen orthophosphate, *tri*Calcium diorthophosphate
296	DL-Malic acid, L-Malic acid		
297	Fumaric acid		

ANTIOXIDANTS

E300	L-Ascorbic acid	350	Sodium malate, sodium hydrogen malate
E301	Sodium L-ascorbate		
E302	Calcium L-ascorbate	351	Potassium malate
E304	6-O-Palmitoyl-L-ascorbic acid **(Ascorbyl palmitate)**	352	Calcium malate, calcium hydrogen malate
E306	Extracts of natural origin rich in tocopherols	353	Metatartaric acid
		355	Adipic acid
E307	Synthetic *alpha*-tocopherol	363	Succinic acid
E308	Synthetic *gamma*-tocopherol	370	1,4-Heptonolactone
		375	Nicotinic acid
E309	Synthetic *delta*-tocopherol	380	*tri*Ammonium citrate
E310	Propyl gallate	381	Ammonium ferric citrate
E311	Octyl gallate	385	Calcium disodium ethylenediamine—NNN'N' tetra-acetate **(Calcium disodium EDTA)**
E312	Dodecyl gallate		
E320	Butylated hydroxyanisole **(BHA)**		
E321	Butylated hydroxytoluene **(BHT)**		
E322	Lecithins		
E325	Sodium lactate		
E326	Potassium lactate		
E327	Calcium lactate		
E330	Citric acid		

►

EMULSIFIERS, STABILIZERS, THICKENERS AND GELLING AGENTS

E400	Alginic acid
E401	Sodium alginate
E402	Potassium alginate
E403	Ammonium alginate
E404	Calcium alginate
E405	Propane-1,2-diol alginate **(Propylene glycol alginate)**
E406	Agar
E407	Carrageenan
E410	Locust bean gum **(Carob gum)**
E412	Guar gum
E413	Tragacanth
E414	Gum arabic **(Acacia)**
E415	Xanthan gum
416	Karaya gum
E420	Sorbitol, sorbitol syrup
E421	Mannitol
E422	Glycerol
430	Polyoxyethylene (8) stearate
431	Polyoxyethylene (40) stearate
432	Polyoxyethylene (20) sorbitan monolaurate **(Polysorbate 20)**
433	Polyoxyethylene (20) sorbitan mono-oleate **(Polysorbate 80)**
434	Polyoxyethylene (20) sorbitan monopalmitate **(Polysorbate 40)**
435	Polyoxyethylene (20) sorbitan monostearate **(Polysorbate 60)**
436	Polyoxyethylene (20) sorbitan tristearate **(Polysorbate 65)**
E440(a)	Pectin
E440(b)	Amidated pectin
442	Ammonium phosphatides
E450(a)	*di*Sodium dihydrogen diphosphate, *tri*Sodium diphosphate, *tetra*Sodium diphosphate, *tetra*Potassium diphosphate
E450(b)	*penta*Sodium triphosphate, *penta*Potassium triphosphate
E450(c)	Sodium polyphosphates, Potassium polyphosphates
E460	Microcrystalline cellulose, *Alpha*-cellulose **(Powdered cellulose)**
E461	Methylcellulose
E463	Hydroxypropylcellulose
E464	Hydroxypropylmethyl-cellulose
E465	Ethylmethylcellulose
E466	Carboxymethylcellulose, sodium salt **(CMC)**
E470	Sodium, potassium and calcium salts of fatty acids
E471	Mono- and di-glycerides of fatty acids
E472(a)	Acetic acid esters of mono- and di-glycerides of fatty acids
E472(b)	Lactic acid esters of mono- and di-glycerides of fatty acids **(Lactoglycerides)**
E472(c)	Citric acid esters of mono- and di-glycerides of fatty acids **(Citroglycerides)**
E472(e)	Mono- and diacetyltartaric acid esters of mono- and di-glycerides of fatty acids
E473	Sucrose esters of fatty acids
E474	Sucroglycerides
E475	Polyglycerol esters of fatty acids
476	Polyglycerol esters of polycondensed fatty acids of castor oil **(Polyglycerol polyricinoleate)**
E477	Propane-1,2-diol esters of fatty acids
478	Lactylated fatty acid esters of glycerol and propane-1,2-diol
E481	Sodium stearoyl-2-lactylate
E482	Calcium stearoyl-2-lactylate
E483	Stearyl tartrate
491	Sorbitan monostearate
492	Sorbitan tristearate
493	Sorbitan monolaurate
494	Sorbitan mono-oleate
495	Sorbitan monopalmitate

MISCELLANEOUS

(Includes flavour enhancers, anti-foaming agents, glazing agents, raising agents, etc.)

500	Sodium carbonate, Sodium hydrogen carbonate **(Bicarbonate of soda),** Sodium sesquicarbonate
501	Potassium carbonate, Potassium hydrogen carbonate
503	Ammonium carbonate, Ammonium hydrogen carbonate
504	Magnesium carbonate
507	Hydrochloric acid
508	Potassium chloride
509	Calcium chloride
510	Ammonium chloride
513	Sulphuric acid
514	Sodium sulphate
515	Potassium sulphate
516	Calcium sulphate
518	Magnesium sulphate
524	Sodium hydroxide
525	Potassium hydroxide
526	Calcium hydroxide
527	Ammonium hydroxide
528	Magnesium hydroxide
529	Calcium oxide
530	Magnesium oxide
535	Sodium ferrocyanide **(Sodium hexacyanoferrate (II))**
536	Potassium ferrocyanide **(Potassium hexacyanoferrate (II))**
540	*di*Calcium diphosphate
541	Sodium aluminium phosphate
542	Edible bone phosphate
544	Calcium polyphosphates
545	Ammonium polyphosphates
551	Silicon dioxide **(Silica)**
552	Calcium silicate
553(a)	Magnesium silicate synthetic, Magnesium trisilicate
553(b)	Talc
554	Aluminium sodium silicate
556	Aluminium calcium silicate
558	Bentonite
559	Kaolin
570	Stearic acid
572	Magnesium stearate
575	D-Glucono-1,5-lactone **(Glucono *delta*-lactone)**
576	Sodium gluconate
577	Potassium gluconate
578	Calcium gluconate
620	L-glutamic acid
621	Sodium hydrogen L-glutamate **(*mono*Sodium glutamate or MSG)**
622	Potassium hydrogen L-glutamate **(*mono*Potassium glutamate)**
623	Calcium dihydrogen di-L-glutamate **(Calcium glutamate)**
627	Guanosine 5′-(disodium phosphate) **(Sodium guanylate)**
631	Inosine 5′-(disodium phosphate) **(Sodium inosinate)**
635	Sodium 5′-ribonucleotide
636	Maltol
637	Ethyl maltol
900	Dimethylpolysiloxane
901	Beeswax
903	Carnauba wax
904	Shellac
905	Mineral hydrocarbons
907	Refined microcrystalline wax
920	L-cysteine hydrochloride
924	Potassium bromate
925	Chlorine
926	Chlorine dioxide
927	Azodicarbonamide **(Azoformamide)**

APPENDIX 3

▶ GCSE CORE CONTENT INDEX

This index is based on the Core Content of the GCSE National Criteria for Chemistry. It lists the question numbers against those aspects of the Core Content with which they are most concerned. Since the Core Content specifies only a minimum, some questions go beyond the Core. To make the index more useful in this respect, such aspects are printed in *italics*.

Experiments
This is not a book of practical work, so most of the experimental skills are not developed, except within the two categories listed below.
Designing experiments   2, 3, 6, 9, 14, 17, 18, 19, 20, 22, 25, 34, 35, 42, 49, 55, 56, 60, 63, 65, 66, 70, 80, 93
Simple tests for common ions and molecules   5, 7, 8, 15, 35, 48

Elements and compounds
H   33, 74, 84
He, Ne, Ar   27, 63, 71
Na, K   31, 35, 58, 65, 92
Mg, Ca   26, 67
Al   91
C, *Si*   60, 81, 84
N   63, 71, 93
O, S   33, 72
Cl, Br, I   30, 46, 50, 53, 55
Fe, Cu, Zn   15, 22, 23, 25, 29, 56

Ideas, models, patterns and theories
Solids, liquids, gases (kinetic theory)   2, 3, 20, 23, 41, 45, 47, 50, 56, 84, 88
Pure substances and mixtures (solutions and solubility; purification; separation)   3, 4, 5, 9, 13, 14, 16, 21, 44, 55, 63, 65, 74
Elements and compounds   13, 25, 63, 67, 86
Metallic and non-metallic characteristics   6, 15, 22, 23, 29, 56, 58, 84, 91
Reactivity series   22, 23, 56, 75, 84, 91
The periodic table   10, 33, 64, 66, 76, 78, 83, 84, 87, 88
Acids, bases and salts   4, 11, 17, 19, 23, 31, 47, 50, 60, 68, 69, 70, 75, 81
pH   18, 48, 50, 51, 55, 63, 71
Atomic structure, bonding (and related properties)   52, 64, 66, 73, 75, 76, 83, 87, 88, 89
Radioactivity (α-, β-decay; half-life)   85, 86, 87, 89

►